Chicken Soup for the Soul®

Kids IN THE KITCHEN

Tasty Recipes and Fun Activities
for Budding Chefs

Jack Canfield, Mark Victor Hansen, and Chef Antonio Frontera

Health Communications, Inc.
Deerfield Beach, Florida

www.hcibooks.com
www.chickensoup.com

We would like to acknowledge the following publishers and individuals for permission to reprint the following material.

A Recipe for Love. Reprinted by permission of Matthew Rahuba and Maria Rahuba. ©2006 Matthew Rahuba.

Tokens of Love. Reprinted by permission of Tessa Lynn Floehr. ©2006 Tessa Lynn Floehr.

Batter Up, Kid. Reprinted by permission of Cristy Trandahl. ©2006 Cristy Trandahl.

Breakfast by the River. Reprinted by permission of Meredith Greenwood Knight. ©1998 Meredith Greenwood Knight.

My First Cooking Lesson. Reprinted by permission of Catherine Inscore. ©2006 Catherine Inscore.

Sandwiches to the Rescue. Reprinted by permission of Gail Endelman Small. ©2006 Gail Endelman Small.

(Continued on page 241)

Library of Congress Cataloging-in-Publication Data

Canfield, Jack, 1944–
  Chicken soup for the soul : kids in the kitchen : tasty recipes and fun activities for budding chefs / Jack Canfield, Mark Victor Hansen, and Antonio Frontera.
    p. cm.
  ISBN-13: 978-0-7573-0579-5 (trade paper)
  ISBN-10: 0-7573-0579-2 (trade paper)
  1. Cookery—Juvenile literature. 2. Children—Anecdotes—Juvenile literature. I. Hansen, Mark Victor. II. Frontera, Antonio. III. Title.

TX652.5.C324 2007
641.5—dc22   2007020559

Publisher: Health Communications, Inc.
        3201 S.W. 15th Street
        Deerfield Beach, FL 33442-8190

Cover and interior book design by Lawna Patterson Oldfield
Photos ©HCI, ©Photos.com, ©Liquid Library, ©PhotoDisc

CONTENTS

PART ONE: BREAKFAST

Part Two: Lunch

Part Three: Dinner

PART FOUR: DESSERTS

ACKNOWLEDGMENTS

We wish to express our heartfelt gratitude to the following people who helped make this book possible.

Our families, who have been chicken soup for our souls!

Jack's Family: Inga, Travis, Riley, Christopher, Oran, and Kyle, for all their love and support.

Mark's Family: Patty, Elisabeth, and Melanie Hansen, for once again sharing and lovingly supporting us in creating yet another book.

Antonio's Family: Thank you, Valeri Frontera and Melchiorre, for giving me life and teaching me about family values. Thanks to Matthew, Ashleigh, Gianna, Giovanni, and all the kids in my life who remind me how precious kids and family are.

Publisher Peter Vegso, for his vision and commitment to bringing *Chicken Soup for the Soul* to the world.

Patty Aubery and Russ Kalmaski, for being there on every step of the journey, with love, laughter, and endless creativity.

Barbara LoMonaco, for nourishing us with truly wonderful stories and cartoons.

D'ette Corona for being there to answer any questions along the way.

Patty Hansen, for her thorough and competent handling of the legal and licensing aspects of the Chicken Soup for the Soul books. You are magnificent at the challenge!

Veronica Romero, Lisa Williams, Teresa Collett, Robin Yerian, Jesse Ianniello, Lauren Edelstein, Lauren Bray, Debbie Lefever, Connie Simoni, Karen Schoenfeld, Marty Robinson, Debbie Lefever, Patti Coffey, Pat Burns, Kristi Waite, and Blake Arce who support Jack's and Mark's businesses with skill and love.

Michele Matrisciani, Carol Rosenberg, Andrea Gold, Allison Janse, Katheline St. Fort, our editors at Health Communications, Inc., for their devotion to excellence.

Terry Burke, Tom Sand, Lori Golden, Kelly Johnson Maragni, Patricia McConnell, Kim Weiss, Paola Fernandez-Rana, the marketing, sales, and PR departments at Health Communications, Inc., for doing such an incredible job supporting our books.

Tom Sand, Claude Choquette, and Luc Jutras, who manage year after year to get our books transferred into thirty-six languages around the world.

Everybody in the art department at Health Communications, Inc., for their talent, creativity, and unrelenting patience in producing book covers and inside designs that capture the essence of Chicken Soup: Larissa Hise Henoch, Lawna Patterson Oldfield, Andrea Perrine Brower, Anthony Clausi, Dawn Von Strolley Grove, and Peter Quintal.

The staff at Antonio Frontera Media for their loyalty: Andrew J. Corsa, Frank Valenza, who has been there every step of the way; Pam Stensgard, Jennifer Chandler, Frank Crocitto, Mark Wilk, Maria Rahuba, Kelly Youngs-Schmidt, Susan Rizzo, and Gail Small, who have contributed in their own special way; and to all the taste testers. Thanks to Jeff Hartford and Golds Gym of the Hudson Valley for their great help with nutrition.

Our glorious panel of readers who helped us make the final selections and made invaluable suggestions on how to improve the book: Valeri Frontera, Maria Rahuba, Gail Small, Andrew Corsa, Mark Wilk, Susan Rizzo, Arlene Uribe, Matthew Rahuba, Carrie Albright, Jana Clay, Jacqueline Hall, Janis Gangi, and Pam Stensgard.

To everyone who submitted a story, we deeply appreciate your letting us into your lives and sharing your experiences with us. For those whose stories were not chosen for publication, we hope the stories you are about to enjoy convey what was in your heart and in some ways also tell your stories.

Because of the size of this project, we may have left out the names of some people who contributed along the way. If so, we are sorry, but please know that we really do appreciate you very much.

We are truly grateful and love you all!

FOREWORD

Hey y'all, it's time to get your family back to the dinner table. It seems that we have made life so complicated that we have forgotten what it's like to have a real family meal. It's almost as if we have lost an entire generation to fast foods. Just think of all that lost opportunity to be with your family.

There is no better way to strengthen family ties than to cook and eat together. It's the one time of the day when you can relax with your kids, hear about their day, and show them how they can contribute to the family meal. It does not have to be complicated. Just bring the kids into the kitchen and show them how to be creative. You would be surprised how much fun it can be.

In addition to strengthening family ties, cooking meals at home gives parents more control over the quality and quantity of foods. Studies show that children who eat meals with their families do better in school and eat more nutritiously. It's also important to know that cooking with your children will teach them important life and social skills.

Antonio Frontera and the Chicken Soup for the Soul family understand the needs of today's modern family. In *Chicken Soup for the Soul Kids in the Kitchen,* Antonio shares wonderful stories and memories about family life and more important, easy and delicious recipes that you can make with your children. This book is filled with lots of great ideas that will make your family's experience in the kitchen fun.

Cooking with your family is the best way to make happy memories and have fun. The important thing is to be together. I am sure that you will enjoy the great stories and recipes in this book. More important, I hope it inspires you to create your own stories and memories.

Best dishes,
Paula Deen

INTRODUCTION

I remember the days when I was just a little boy watching my grandmother make pasta by hand. I remember the look on her face and how happy cooking for her family made her. She rolled every piece of pasta by hand and put it on her pasta table to dry all day. (Yes, back then, they had a table just to dry the pasta.) Those days were great. I also have fond memories of my family enjoying all of the food my grandmother prepared.

I was fortunate enough to be around a family who loved to cook. We lived only minutes from one another, and I went from house to house and observed the skill and love that went into every dish. I went from Grandma Yolanda to Grandpa Joe, who was a baker by trade. Believe me, he could bake, and to this day, my family still bakes his famous cookies. The person who really taught me the art of cooking was my mother, Valerie. She cooked every day. I used to look forward to snow days so I could stay home from school and cook and bake with her all day. I still love cooking with her. In fact, I love cooking and eating with all of my relatives.

It disheartens me when kids tell me they never cook with their family members and rarely eat with them. So, along with my coauthors, I decided to bring children and their families back into the kitchen with *Chicken Soup for the Soul Kids in the Kitchen.* This book will inspire family bonding, cherished memories, and a whole lot of cooking fun. I would like to see families get back into the kitchen and talk together, eat together, enjoy one another's company, laugh, and have a good time—all the things we're often missing in the world today.

In this book, you will learn the basics of measuring and cooking while sharing special moments you will cherish for the rest of your lives. So, take a voyage with Chicken Soup for the Soul and me and create and have fun. In many ways, I am still living my childhood days through my cooking. You, too, can fall in love with cooking and make it a lifelong career or, at the very least, a lifetime of wonderful memories.

—*Chef Antonio Frontera*

My Top Ten Favorite Foods

Chef Antonio has placed his **Top Ten Favorite Foods** throughout this book for you to find. They are numbered from 1 to 10. Go ahead now and find them, and then list them below, according to your own likes. Join Chef Antonio on a scavenger hunt and let's have some fun!

#1 _____

#2 _____

#3 _____

#4 _____

#5 _____

#6 _____

#7 _____

#8 _____

#9 _____

#10 _____

Let's Get Started!
Some "Must Knows"

All Right Boys and Girls! Before we start there are some very important things you must know. Safety is a major part of cooking. You can get hurt, so listen up and pay attention to these very important kitchen rules. Cooking is not that hard, so go ahead and cook, be safe, and have fun.

—Antonio Frontera

Safety

1. Always ask adults for help, especially when you heat anything.

2. Dry your hands before plugging in or using any electrical appliance.

3. Whenever dealing with anything heated, use clean, dry pot holders or oven mitts. Cooking is fun, but you do need to be careful.

4. I cannot stress this important rule enough: *Never, ever, ever* put knives, or *anything* that cuts, into the sink. Every time you finish using a knife, wash it and put it back in the safe place where it belongs.

5. Do not put anything metal inside a microwave oven! When using a microwave oven, make sure you use glass, ceramic, or plastic containers that are approved for a microwave. Remember to use pot holders when removing plates and bowls from the microwave, since any dish can become very hot!

> **FUN FACT:**
> Average food consumption per person is 1,500 pounds per year. Eat wisely!

6. When cooking, never leave food unattended. Always make sure someone is in the room and paying attention.

7 Do not leave pot handles positioned so that someone could bump into them and get hurt. Keep pot handles "turned in" on the stovetop and other surfaces.

Safe Cooking

1 Wash your hands *before* handling any type of food. Wash your hands *between* handling different types of raw and uncooked foods.

2 Always keep raw meat, fish, poultry, and eggs in the refrigerator.

3 Do not let raw meat, fish, or eggs touch any of your cooked foods. Keep these raw foods away from every other type of food.

4 Don't break eggs directly into the food you are preparing. Always break them into a separate bowl or cup, and then add them to your recipe. That way, you can avoid adding shells or other undesirable elements to your food.

5 Wash cutting boards with warm, soapy water after each use. This is particularly important if you are cutting raw meat.

6 Always wash fresh vegetables and fruits before using them.

7 Use different work spaces and cutting boards for different types of food. Do not use the same cutting board and work space for raw meat, poultry, and other foods.

Keeping Clean and Organized

1 Make sure you have all the tools and ingredients you will need to finish your recipe.

2 Have utensils and ingredients ready for use and know where they are. Stay organized and ready!

3 Clean up as you go. Remember, cooking is fun, not a chore. If you spill something, clean it up. We don't want anyone to slip and fall.

4 If you make a mistake, don't feel bad. Every chef makes mistakes. Learn from your mistakes. Remember, cooking is fun!

Culinary Math

Measuring Big Amounts

1 cup = 8 fluid ounces

1 pint = 2 cups or 16 fluid ounces

1 quart = 4 cups or 32 fluid ounces

1 gallon = 16 cups or 128 fluid ounces

Measuring Small Amounts

½ tablespoon = 1½ teaspoons

1 tablespoon = 3 teaspoons

2 tablespoons = 1 fluid ounce

16 tablespoons = 1 cup

Weight (Mass)

1 gram = 1,000 milligrams

1 ounce = 28.35 grams

1 kilogram = 2.21 pounds

Volume (Liquid)

1 liter = 33.8 fluid ounces

1 cup = ¼ liter

1 quart = 1 liter

1 ounce = 30 grams

8 ounces = 240 grams

Meat Temperatures

Rare = 120°F–130°F

Medium Rare = 130°F–140°F

Medium = 140°F–150°F

Medium Well = 150°F–160°F

Well = 160°F–165°F

Cooking Terms

Bake: To cook something so that the heat comes from all around the food.

Beat: To mix something quickly with force.

Blend: To mix completely, until smooth.

Boil: To heat water until it bubbles.

Broil: To cook something so that the heat comes from above the food.

Grate: To rub against a grater; a utensil with holes in it.

Grease: To add a thin coating of a shortening (butter, grease, oil).

Knead: To push, turn, press, and fold dough with your hands.

Marinate: To soak in a liquid to tenderize or enrich the flavor of meat and poultry.

Peel: To remove the outer skin.

Preheat: To heat something before you are ready to use it. You typically preheat something 10 to 15 minutes before you use it.

Simmer: To heat to a light, slow bubble.

Whip: To mix ingredients at a high speed, adding air to the food.

Cooking Utensils

✓ Baking dish

✓ Cutting board

✓ Baking sheet

✓ Electric Mixer

✓ Basting brush

✓ Frying pan

✓ Blender

✓ Food processor

✓ Casserole dish

✓ Grater

✓ Colander

✓ Knives

✓ Cooling rack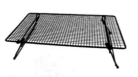

✓ Ladle

Cooking Utensils *(continued)*

✓ Measuring cups

✓ Saucepan

✓ Measuring spoons

✓ Skillet

✓ Mixing bowls

✓ Spatula

✓ Muffin tin

✓ Spoon

✓ Oven mitt

✓ Vegetable Peeler

✓ Potato masher

✓ Whisk

✓ Rolling pin

A Sneak Peek into Nutrition

Have you ever wondered where you get the energy to play with your friends, read a book, or play computer games? Well, it all starts with nutrition. You get important nutrients from the foods that you eat and the better the food like fruits, vegetables, and whole grains, the better the nutrition. One of the reasons I wrote this book was to share some of my family recipes and the nutrients that helped me get through school and live a healthy life.

A Note from Golds Gym

Let's start by paying more attention to what it means to be healthy. Did you eat breakfast this morning? While you slept, your body used up a lot of its stored energy, and it needs new energy to start the day off right. Where does energy come from? The sun! And how do we get energy from the sun into our bodies? Food! And the better the food we eat, the more energy we get! Some of the foods that have lots of energy from the sun include plants like leafy green vegetables, seeds, and nuts like almonds and sunflower seeds, whole grains, and quality meat and dairy. What'd you have for lunch? Did you eat dinner? Where did the food you ate today come from? Did it come from the ground? From a cow? From a tree? Did it come from the ocean? It's fun to see!

All of this good food gives us energy for exercise, and exercise helps keep our muscles and bones strong and healthy! Playing kickball at recess, playing tag, swimming, dancing, riding bikes or scooters—these are all forms of exercise. Walking the dog is exercise, too! Can you name an exercise that you like to do? Getting or staying healthy is up to you in the choices that you make every-day—in the types of food you eat and the exercise that you do, and in the amount of rest you get. So let's make sure you are eating the right foods and getting enough exercise, so you, too, can be healthy and feel good—for the rest of your life!

Golds Gym of the Hudson Valley

What are nutrients?

They are substances in foods that are needed for you to grow and repair and keep your body healthy.

What are the three main nutrients?

1. **Proteins:** These are needed for your body to grow strong and healthy.

2. **Carbohydrates:** These are the starches and sugars in food that provide much of the energy the body needs to work and play. Carbohydrates also contain fiber.

3. **Fats:** These supply more energy for your body than any other nutrient. They also help in cell building and oxygen transport. They are necessary for flavoring and creating a sense of fullness.

What about food groups?

There are five main food groups, plus fats and oils.

What are these five food groups?

1. Meat, poultry, fish, beans, eggs, and nuts

2. Fruit

3. Grains and starches

4. Dairy

5. Vegetables

Is there any way to cook besides frying?

Well, of course there are many tasty and nutritious ways of cooking.

Healthy Cooking Methods

- **Poaching:** To cook in water with a shallow amount of liquid at a low boiling point.

- **Broiling:** To cook foods at a high temperature from an overhead heat source.

- **Grilling:** To cook on a grate or on anything that has openings over a heat source.

- **Stir-frying:** To fry quickly in a lightly oiled pan while stirring continuously. (To make stir-fry in a more healthy way, use the spray oils.)

- **Steaming:** To cook with steam generated by a heated liquid.

- **Roasting:** To cook food by surrounding it with dry heat. (When roasting in a healthy way, do not add any additional fats. Use a rack in the roasting pan, and make sure you always drain off any excess fat.)

What is healthy eating?

Home-cooked meats are better than processed meats.

Eat snacks with egg whites rather than whole eggs.

Applesauce is a good substitute for sugar, and so is fruit.

Leave the fat aside, and use skim milk rather than whole milk.

Take out the white flour and use whole wheat.

Help yourself to baked foods rather than fried foods.

Yogurt can be used instead of cream.

1 BREAKFAST

Ready—Set—GO!

*"When you rise in the morning and smell
the aroma coming from the kitchen, you know at
that moment it will be a glorious day."*

—Chef Antonio Frontera

You can't go too far when you are out of gas. ***You need fuel! Power! Nutrients!***

If an empty car sleeps all night long, how far can it go in the morning? If it doesn't fill up, it will be slow and sluggish, and it will finally shut down. If you sleep all night, and don't fill up in the morning, you'll be slow and sluggish, too!

People are always telling me that I should eat a good breakfast! They're right! Eat something, but don't eat just sugar and fat, because sugar and fat won't help you get through your day. You will still run out of gas.

Breakfast is about new beginnings, new hope, and the promise of a new day. No two days are ever the same, so enjoy and explore. Get fueled and get powered. Be a believer in breakfast because it does make a difference. That's the root of the expression "Breakfast of Champions." And everyone can be a champion!

Breakfast is the first meal you eat when you wake up after a night of sleeping and fasting. In fact, "breakfast" is a compound word: break-fast. You are breaking your fast and giving nourishment to an empty stomach so you can energize yourself.

Worldwide, eating breakfast is considered the healthy way to begin a new day. It's a gift to your body. There are many kinds of breakfast you can try because breakfasts are different throughout the world in many families, regions, and countries. Learning about the breakfasts of different cultures might make you curious about other people and their traditions.

Did you have cereal for breakfast today? Was it hot or cold? Did you know that it is called "porridge" in some places in the world? Do you sometimes like peanut butter on toast? In Australia, some love Vegemite, not peanut butter.

You can learn all about foreign foods. You might even try them one day! I will share breakfast foods that I know about, and you can find others to add to the list: rice, soup, fish, noodles, peas, chutney, cheese, bagels, croissants, yogurt, sandwiches, and more.

Lots of people eat eggs for breakfast. Eggs can be made in many different ways, such as poached, scrambled, fried, over easy, over hard, or as an omelet.

There are many breakfast alternatives: hot breakfast, cold breakfast, or something freshly made, from a package, or put together the night before to save time in the morning. You can eat breakfast in a chair or on the run, on a plate, in a cup, or in a bag. Count the number of foods you can eat for breakfast. There are so many possibilities. You can be creative, and you can look forward to breakfast.

Now think about this: next time you can't sleep, don't count sheep—count ways of making breakfasts!

—*Chef Antonio Frontera*

A RECIPE FOR LOVE

🛒 INGREDIENTS

- ♥ A little pinch of this,
- ♥ A little cup of that,
- ♥ A dab of care,
- ♥ And a tiny kiss,
- ♥ A large hug,
- ♥ And a whole bunch of special moments.

🍹 TOOLS

- ♥ Arms
- ♥ Heart
- ♥ Lips
- ♥ Mind
- ♥ Soul

DIRECTIONS

1 BLEND all the ingredients until smooth.

2 PUT the mixture in your heart.

3 KEEP it in mind.

4 SERVE, with the warmth of love, to your family.

—Chef Antonio Frontera with
Matthew Rahuba

TOKENS OF LOVE

Whenever I bite into a warm chocolate-chip pancake, a feeling of comfort and love fills me as I remember my mom's special breakfasts. You see, my mom was not a morning person, so my typical before-school nutrition was cold cereal and milk. But if I had a big test or an important event (like a spelling bee or an oral report), I would wake up to the sweet aroma of chocolate and pancakes floating through the house. On those special days, Mom would set her alarm so she could whip up some of her special mini chocolate-chip pancakes to give me an extra boost before school. I always felt pampered and cherished on those mornings. I can still picture my mom in her worn blue robe with sleep still in her eyes, standing over the pan with a spatula in hand ready to flip those tokens of her love at just the right time.

My mom passed away a few years ago, but I still feel connected to her in so many ways. A warm chocolate-chip pancake can transport me back to my childhood and help me recall my mom's way of making me feel special and loved.

Sometimes when I am feeling lonely and missing Mom, I'll mix up a bowl of batter and make a batch of chocolate-chip pancakes for my daughters and myself. As I stand by the pan, ready to flip the pancakes, I think of my mom and how much her special breakfasts meant to me.

I have carried on this tradition with my two daughters, making sure that important days always start with an extraspecial breakfast. This extra labor of love in the morning helps me not only fill my girls' bellies with nutritious food but also fill their souls with a warm feeling of love and value before they head out into the world—just like I felt after eating my mom's tokens of love so many years ago.

—*Tessa Floehr*

MoM's chocoLaTe-chiP PaNCaKeS

Wow! These taste like big chocolate-chip cookies, just like Mom makes, right out of the oven.

SERVES 4–6

🛒 INgReDieNTS

- 2 cups all-purpose flour
- 1 teaspoon baking powder
- 1 teaspoon baking soda
- 1⅓ cups milk
- 1 egg
- 2 tablespoons sugar
- 1 teaspoon vanilla
- ½ cup semisweet chocolate chips
- Nonstick cooking spray
- Pancake syrup, *optional*

🍴 TooLS

Mixing bowl

Measuring cup

Measuring spoons

Mixing spoon

Skillet

Pancake turner

> 💡 **TIP:**
> For a fluffier pancake,
> substitute seltzer for all
> or half of the milk.

DIRECTIONS

1 **IN** a mixing bowl, stir together all the ingredients, except the chocolate chips and nonstick cooking spray, until smooth. Then gently stir in the chocolate chips.

2 **SPRAY** a skillet with the nonstick cooking spray and heat it over medium heat for a few minutes. Ladle some of the batter into the skillet, depending on the size of the skillet and using approximately ¼ cup of batter for each pancake. Cook until bubbles form on the surface and then flip the pancake. Cook for another minute or so (until the top and the bottom of the pancake are both golden brown).

3 **SERVE** with or without syrup.

BaTTeR, UP, KiD

*P*ancakes! Oh my gosh! I had forgotten about my daughter's pancake endeavor.

Spinning around like a lazy Susan, I spotted my little seven-year-old mixing her first batch of pancakes. So many, many, pancakes! "Oh, honey, no!" I cried, fumbling for the family-size box of instant pancake mix she held suspended over an overflowing mixing bowl.

"Is this enough for the whole family, Mom?" My daughter smiled, with batter, like bird droppings, plopped on her chubby cheeks. Her long, blond hair was encrusted with thick mix; her tan arms dripped white with the sticky stuff. Puddles of pancake batter, a gooey, gluey slush, clung to the counters.

I could have cried. Twice. I wanted to bang my head against the syrup-smeared cupboards and yell at someone. Anyone.

Instead of yelling, I smiled and said, "Good for you, honey! You did it! You made enough pancakes for the whole family. And you did it yourself."

That morning, our family consumed twenty-two pancakes. We froze a dozen, donated four to our hungry dog, and we still had batter to spare.

Today, my eldest daughter, that sweet seven-year-old chef, is a teenager. Soon, she will learn to drive, graduate high school, choose a college, and move away from home. She will make mistakes—mistakes way bigger than the pancake batter blunder. After all, a few lumps always remain in the batter of life.

I only hope and pray that, as my daughter matures and chooses her own recipe for her future, I can conjure up the image of that beautiful, batter-splattered little girl. If I can overcome my own fear and pride, I'll be able to tell my daughter, in any situation, "Good for you, honey. Go ahead and try it. You can do this all by yourself."

—*Cristy Trandahl*

OaTMeaL-RaisiN COOKiE PaNCaKES

Who said you can't eat cookies for breakfast? I made this up when I was a kid so I could have a cookie with my breakfast. You will be getting your oatmeal in as well!

INGReDieNTS

- 1 cup quick-cooking oats
- 1 cup buttermilk
- 1 cup milk
- ½ cup plus ½ cup club soda
- 2 eggs
- ½ cup butter, melted
- ½ cup all-purpose flour
- 2 tablespoons sugar
- 2 tablespoons brown sugar
- 2 teaspoons baking powder
- ½ teaspoon ground cinnamon
- ½ cup raisins
- ½ teaspoon salt
- Nonstick cooking spray
- Cinnamon butter, *optional*
- Chocolate chips, *optional*

TOOLS

Mixing bowl

Mixing spoon

Measuring cup

Measuring spoons

Griddle or frying pan

Pancake turner

Ladle

SERVES 4

☼ TIP:
Why do we use club soda?
To make it light and fluffy!

☼ TIP: You can top these pancakes with cinnamon butter and you are all set. Or you can use chocolate chips instead of raisins to make the ultimate oatmeal chocolate chip cookie dough pancakes. Yum, yum!

DiRecTioNS

1 **IN** a mixing bowl, combine the oats, buttermilk, and milk. Let the mixture stand for about 10 minutes; then add the eggs and melted butter.

2 **ADD** ½ cup of club soda, and then add the flour, sugar, brown sugar, baking powder, cinnamon, raisins, and salt. Stir, then add the remaining ½ cup of club soda. Stir again until all ingredients are mixed.

3 **SPRay** a griddle or frying pan with the nonstick cooking spray and heat it over medium heat for a few minutes. Ladle some of the batter into the skillet, depending on the size of the skillet and using approximately ¼ cup of batter for each pancake. Cook until bubbles form on the surface and then flip the pancake. Cook for another minute or so (until the top and the bottom of the pancake are both golden brown).

Breakfast by The River

It was almost dusk as I walked down the trail at the back of our property with my eight-year-old daughter, Haley, and my three-year-old son, Hewson. "I've got a great idea," I announced. "Let's come out here, first thing in the morning, and have our breakfast by the river."

My children loved the idea. "The second we open our eyes," I promised, "we'll go to the river before we do anything else!" Before I went to bed, I packed a breakfast of muffins and grape juice, thinking, *I'm not always the fun mom I want to be, but I do have my moments.*

All of us have an idea, before we have kids, of the kind of parent we hope to be. As for me, I hoped I was always going to see the big picture. I would never get so bogged down with housework and day-to-day details that I'd forget to cherish every minute with my kids. Of course, eight years later I find myself getting bogged down. Too often, getting dinner on the table takes precedence over reading a book to Hewson. I find myself engrossed in a project and groan when I hear my six-year-old, Molly, take a tumble, knowing that I'll have to stop long enough to kiss away the boo-boo. I even hear myself speaking the words I swore I'd never say: "Hurry! Hurry! Hurry!" Far too many nights, I lie in bed thinking back over the impatient, intolerant mom I have become and think, *Well, that's certainly not the mom I thought I'd be!*

But after recommending breakfast by the river, I smiled and thought, *Now this is more like it. When I open my eyes, I will gather my three children. We'll walk hand in hand to the river where we'll sit, and I'll tell them stories about when I was little. I'll be witty and lighthearted, and they'll look back on this day, years from now, and think how lucky they are to have a mom like me.*

Morning came a little too soon for Molly. When she entered my room, I opened one eye and peeked at the clock. It was 6:00 AM. Too early for this fun-loving mom. I didn't get up. Instead, I directed her to sleep on a small pallet I keep on the side of my bed for just such occasions. Next in the room was Hewson. I played possum until he slipped under the covers between his dad and me and fell back to sleep.

The next thing I knew, it was 7:30, and Haley was in the room, booming, "Come on, Mom. Remember! We're going to the river for breakfast." Molly, who'd been asleep when our plan was made, asked, "Why are we going to the river?"

"Oh, you're not going. Just me, Mom, and Hewson," Haley explained.

This launched them into a major squabble, which I calmed while trying to shake myself awake.

I made it to the kitchen, where I grabbed the coffeepot to pour myself a cup, only to discover that the automatic brew feature wasn't so automatic after all. I groaned, turned the knob to "on," and hollered at my girls. "Run and put on some shoes," I said, hoping to buy enough time to brew myself a cup.

Of course, without Mom's help no one could find the shoes they wanted. *Let's just go already,* I thought as I searched under beds for sneakers.

I grabbed Hewson's slip-on shoes and lifted him onto the counter so I could put them on his feet. In that special way all three-year olds have, he insisted that I change his slip-ons to boots, his boots to tennis shoes, and his tennis shoes back to slip-ons.

The girls plunged into another skirmish, and I tried to referee. It was ten minutes since we'd gotten up, and we were no closer to leaving the house. I heard my husband, David, start the shower and contemplated climbing back in bed. I thought, *It was a stupid idea! I never wanted to go to the river, anyway!*

Nonetheless, I poured myself coffee and began to gather up the breakfast things. All the while, my children fought to grab my attention.

Haley: "Mom, will you fix me some hot chocolate?"

Molly: "I don't want muffins. I want pop tarts.

Hewson: "I hate these shoes! I want my boots!"

Haley: "If she gets pop tarts, I want waffles."

Their barrage of comments was more than my groggy mind could handle. I grabbed breakfast and my mug of coffee and headed out the back door, leaving it open in case anyone was inclined to follow me.

Moping across the yard, I grumbled to the dog, "That's what I get for trying to be FUN!" I stopped and set my coffee cup on a tree stump so I could retie my shoe. *Kerplunk!* The coffee cup hit the ground and soaked the bottom half of my pajama pants.

Hewson clambered out the back door. "Wait up, Mommy!" I waited, glaring straight ahead. As we entered the woods, Molly and Haley caught up with us. Molly asked, "Mom, why'd you leave us in the kitchen?" I walked straight ahead, ignoring her when she asked, "Did you get my Pop Tarts?" Finally at the river, we settled down on the sand. The dogs found cool spots under the trees. The cat settled into my lap. I began to pour grape juice and opened the muffin tin.

Haley shouted, "Look!" and when we did, we saw a shaft of light cutting through the trees, reflecting on the river, making light patterns all along the other bank.

We saw a fish jump out of the river and splash back into it. That reminded me of a story about my brother and father falling out of their boat on a fishing trip. I began telling the story with great flair. The girls loved it and begged to hear it again.

We started a sand castle and one story led to another. Then, I taught them a song I used to sing at summer camp. We heard footsteps behind us. David had walked back to kiss us "good-bye" before heading to work. As he bent down, he whispered in my ear, "You're a wonderful mom. Our kids are lucky to have you."

I smiled to myself as the kids jumped to kiss Daddy "good-bye."

I have my moments, I thought. *I do have my moments.*

—*Mimi Greenwood Knight*

"Surprise Mommy! I wanted to do something nice for you."

Reprinted by permission of Bruce Robinson. ©2007 Bruce Robinson.

CARROT RAISIN MUFFINS

🛒 INGREDIENTS

- ¼ cup orange juice
- ½ cup skim milk
- ¼ cup vegetable oil
- 2 egg whites
- 2 tablespoons honey
- 1 cup all-purpose flour
- 1 cup whole wheat flour
- 2 teaspoons baking powder
- 1 teaspoon ground cinnamon
- 1 teaspoon orange zest
- 1 cup grated carrots
- 1 cup raisins
- ½ cup crushed pineapple, drained

TOOLS

Large mixing bowl

Measuring cups

Measuring spoons

Mixing spoon

Electric mixer

Muffin tin

12 paper muffin cups

Toothpick

> ☀ **TIP:**
> Go ahead and buy that delicious cream cheese icing in the store and spread it on these delicious muffins.

THINGS THAT MAKE YOU GO "HMMMM":

Carrots really can help you see in the dark.

DIRECTIONS

MAKES
3 DOZEN

1 PREHEAT the oven to 350 degrees.

2 IN a large mixing bowl, combine the orange juice, milk, oil, egg whites, and honey.

3 ADD the flours, baking powder, cinnamon, and orange zest to the liquid mixture. Mix with an electric mixer until blended.

4 ADD the carrots, raisins, and crushed pineapple. Stir until blended.

5 LINE a muffin tin with paper muffin cups, then spoon the mixture into the paper cups until they are about three-quarters full.

6 BAKE for 20 to 25 minutes or until a toothpick inserted in the center comes out clean.

Chocolate Cheesecake Muffins

Makes
2 Dozen

🛒 Ingredients

- 8 ounces cream cheese
- 1 cup sugar divided in half
- ½ cup chocolate chips
- 2 eggs
- ¾ cup milk
- ⅓ cup oil
- 1 cup all-purpose flour
- 4 tablespoons cocoa powder
- 2 teaspoons baking powder
- ½ teaspoon salt
- Chocolate chips, *optional*

Tools

Small mixing bowl

Measuring cups

Measuring spoons

Mixing spoon

Large mixing bowl

Muffin tin

12 paper muffin cups

Toothpick

> ☼ **TIP:** Add some chocolate chips to the cream cheese mixture. Yummy yum yum!

#1 **MUFFIN**—It's not sweet. It's not soft. It's not even pretty to look at. But on those mornings when getting out of bed is so hard, those mornings when you want to hide under the covers and never come out, what's better than a muffin? Eat a big, plump one with bumps on the outside. Eat a lopsided one with funny edges, or maybe a muffin that has blueberries inside. Muffins make us smile. They fill us to the brim. And if they're still warm, they're even more special! Besides, "muffin" is a fun word to say five times in a row—fast!

DiRECTiONS

❶ PREhEaT the oven to 350 degrees.

❷ IN the small mixing bowl, combine cream cheese, half the sugar, chocolate chips, and 1 egg; set aside.

❸ IN the large mixing bowl, combine the remaining egg, milk, and oil. Stir until combined; then add the remaining ½ cup sugar, flour, cocoa powder, baking powder, and salt.

❹ LiNE a muffin tin with the paper muffin cups. Fill each cup three-quarters full with batter, then spoon 1 tablespoon of the cream cheese mixture on top.

❺ BaKE for 20 to 25 minutes or until a toothpick inserted in the center comes out clean.

OMELETS TO GO

hether you're on the move or on the go, pick up an omelet to go! When you're moving quickly, you need quick food, and these really fly!

🛒 INGREDIENTS

- Nonstick cooking spray
- 1 can (approximately 16 ounces) refrigerator biscuits
- 1 pound bacon
- 3 eggs
- 2 cups shredded Cheddar cheese
- 1 tablespoon chopped onion
- ¼ cup mayonnaise
- 2 plum tomatoes, chopped small

🏺 TOOLS

Muffin tin

Frying pan

Mixing bowl

Measuring cups

Measuring spoons

Mixing spoon

Knife

SERVES 4–6

> 👆 **VARIATION:**
> Instead of bacon, use breakfast sausage, ham, onion, or (especially for vegetarians) cooked broccoli.

DiRections

1 **PREHEaT** the oven to 350 degrees.

2 **SPRaY** the muffin tins with the nonstick cooking spray.

3 **TEaR** each biscuit into three equal pieces. Flatten each piece and push three into the bottom of each muffin cup.

4 **COOK** bacon until crisp, then drain and crumble it.

5 **IN** a mixing bowl, mix the eggs, cheese, onion, mayonnaise, and tomatoes with the mixing spoon. Stir in the crumbled bacon.

6 **SPOON** about a tablespoon of the mixture onto each biscuit in the muffin tin.

7 **BaKE** for 10 to 12 minutes, until the eggs are firm.

💡 **TIP:**
You can make these omelets with pie crust instead of biscuit dough.

Frittata

This is an Italian version of the omelet. When Mom cooked this when I was a kid, she always had leftovers in the refrigerator. I would wake up and heat them in the microwave and have a great breakfast without Mom's help.

INGREDIENTS

- 7 eggs
- ¼ teaspoon salt
- ¼ teaspoon pepper
- ¼ cup grated Parmesan cheese
- 1 tablespoon butter
- 8 ounces peas, or other vegetable

TOOLS

Mixing bowl

Measuring spoons

Whisk

Saucepan

Mixing spoon

Spatula

> ☀ **TIP:**
> You can substitute anything you like for peas. Italians have no rules for their delicious omelet!

DIRECTIONS

1 **IN** the mixing bowl, whisk together the eggs, salt, pepper, and cheese.

2 **IN** the saucepan, melt the butter over medium heat. Add the vegetables and heat for 3 minutes.

SERVES
4

3 **STIR** in the egg mixture and cook it on low heat until the eggs are set, stirring occasionally with the spatula. Cover and cook for 10 minutes.

4 **WHEN** the eggs are cooked all the way through, flip the frittata onto a serving plate. Cut and enjoy.

BREAKFAST GRANOLA

I eat this as my cereal in the morning. It's wholesome and beats all those sugary boxed cereals. Tastes yummy, too.

SERVES 4-6

> 💡 **TIP:** One good thing about this delicious granola is that you can customize it to your taste.

🛒 INGREDIENTS

- 6 cups rolled oats
- 1 cup peanuts
- 1 cup almonds
- 1 cup sunflower seeds
- ½ cup yogi berries, *optional*
- ½ cup raisins
- ½ cup dried cranberries
- 1 cup honey
- ½ cup oil

🥤 TOOLS

Mixing bowl

Measuring cups

Mixing spoon

Microwave-safe bowl

Microwave

Baking sheet pan

Spatula

DIRECTIONS

1 PREHEAT the oven to 300 degrees.

2 IN a mixing bowl, combine the oats, peanuts, almonds, sunflower seeds, yogi berries, raisins, and cranberries.

3 WARM the honey and oil in a microwave-safe bowl in a microwave until warm.

4 ADD the honey-oil mixture to the dry ingredients.

5 PLACE the mixture on the baking sheet pan. Bake for 30 minutes. Stir the mixture every 5 minutes to ensure even baking. Cook until lightly browned.

ENJOY IN THE MORNING OR as a SNACK!

Breakfast Burrito

🛒 Ingredients

- 4 slices bacon
- 4 breakfast sausages
- 8 eggs
- ½ teaspoon oil
- 4 flour tortillas
- 1 cup shredded Cheddar cheese
- 8 tablespoons salsa

🧺 Tools

Frying pan

Small mixing bowl

Whisk

Saucepan

Microwave

Serves 4

ENJOY THESE ON THE RUN!

FUN FACT:

A tortilla is a type of unleavened bread generally made from corn. With the introduction of wheat by the Europeans, the flour tortilla was born.

DiRECTiONS

☀ TIP:
You can use corn or flour tortillas.

1 COOK the bacon and sausage in a frying pan until cooked through. Drain and set aside.

2 WhiSK the eggs in the small mixing bowl.

3 HEaT the oil in the saucepan over medium heat. Add the eggs and stir until cooked.

4 HEaT the tortillas in the microwave for 5 seconds each, or until warm.

5 PLaCE each warm tortilla flat on a plate and divide the eggs among them; then add the sausage, bacon, Cheddar cheese, and salsa. Fold up each tortilla around the filling and microwave each for another 10 seconds until hot and the cheese is melted.

My First Cooking Lesson

You are only young once,
so enjoy it and cook up a storm!

—Chef Antonio Frontera

Captain Kangaroo occupied us kids in the front room while Mom tried to catch a few extra winks of sleep. My brothers and sisters were all whining at me. "I'm starving!" cried Cindy. She resembled a roly-poly, curly-headed, Campbell Soup kid.

"Me, too," piped Carol.

There I stood, a lanky five-year old, wanting to solve the problem at hand. My mom was pregnant and tired, and I wanted to surprise her and make breakfast for my brothers and sisters!

I told my siblings to be patient, and I walked into the kitchen, dragging a wobbly stepladder to the kitchen cabinets, I climbed all the way to the top rung. I stretched my small arms until my little fingers could reach one of the big boxes in a cabinet.

I pulled the box out of the cabinet and contemplated it. *This will do,* I thought. My tiny fingers had grabbed a box of round, thin gingersnaps. I thought, *Making these will be just like making pancakes!*

I went right to work. I lugged a heavy, cast-iron frying pan over to the gas range. Then I pulled a box of wooden matches down from above the stove. I swiped a sulfur-blue stick across the rough brown side of the box. The match sizzled, "Schhhht!" I touched the lit match to the gas, and a hot blast of air braised my face.

I dragged the frying pan over the flame, then placed the cookies one by one in the pan. I felt tall and proud, statuesque. My chestnut hair drooped over my eyes as sweat beaded along my thin brows. I worked diligently, trying to flip the cookies.

They were stuck! They would not come off the pan! Smoke permeated the kitchen, the hallway, and the house. The sickening, sweet smell of burning sugar and ginger burned my nose. It smelled horrible! Soon, the atrocious scent penetrated my mother's bedroom.

I heard the bedsprings twang as my mother rose abruptly from her slumber. I thought, *Mom will be so angry if she sees this mess!* Terror slapped me into a corner of the room. Tears flooded my face, stinging behind my eyelids.

My mom flew by me, holding her stomach and her mouth. Furiously, she carried the pan of burnt sugar to the sink and doused the ashen, unrecognizable mass. Then my mother zoomed out of the kitchen and opened every door and window in the house. Finally, she bolted to the toilet. The sounds of her lunging around echoed throughout the house and made me shudder.

I thought, *She's sick! It's all my fault!* Sobbing hard, I said to myself, *I was just trying to help. Mom is going to be so angry!*

I cowered, petrified, frail, and small, in the hallway. My tears became violent. I trembled, and my heart fluttered faster than hummingbird wings. My whitened, tight lips quivered with every teardrop. I slumped to the floor and awaited my punishment.

I heard the toilet flush, and soon my mother entered the kitchen. Her face was green; obviously, the roller coaster in her stomach had not subsided.

My mother swallowed hard and, sighing, stepped to the sink and scrubbed the glop off the pan with a steel-wool pad. Expressionless, she cleaned the stove and never once glanced my way.

She was furious. I just knew it! I plopped my fingernails into my mouth, and I chewed them to the quick!

My mother walked toward me, and I, rolling into an insignificant little ball, tried hard to get out of her way. She passed me and went right for the icebox. Opening the door, she bent over and pulled out eggs and butter. Next, my mom moved to the old breadbox and retrieved a loaf of sliced wheat bread. With her hands securely on her round belly, she halted right smack in front of me and peered at me with a cocked smirk.

My cry changed from sobbing to short, heaving breaths. Quickly, Mom scooped me up into her warm, cozy arms, placed me on my rickety old ladder, dried away my tears with her hand towel, giggled, and said, "Well Cathy, looks like you want a cooking lesson." Softly, she added, "It will be good to have an extra pair of hands in my kitchen."

We worked side by side. With the watchful eyes and loving guidance of my mom, I learned how to make scrambled eggs and toast. From that day on, the kitchen was mine. By age ten, I was preparing full-course meals for twelve or more.

This day is forever welded into my memory: the day my mom treated me like an equal for the first time. From then on, I was to be her right hand in the kitchen and in life.

—*Catherine Inscore*

Eggs Antonio

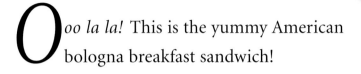

O oo la la! This is the yummy American bologna breakfast sandwich!

🛒 Ingredients

- 4 English muffins, split
- 4 slices bologna
- 4 eggs
- 4 slices American cheese
- Salt and pepper

🖌 Tools

Toaster

Plates

Nonstick frying pan

Spatula

EGG FRESHNESS TEST: Fill a bowl with cold water, add salt, and place the egg in the water. If the egg sinks to the bottom, it is fresh. If it rises to the top, it is no good.

Directions

1 **Toast** the English muffins, then place them on plates.

2 **Heat** the bologna slices in the nonstick frying pan until they are hot on both sides.

SERVES 4

3 **Cook** the eggs the way you like them, and then place them on the bologna slices. Then top each egg with a slice of cheese and the other half of an English muffin.

PEANUT BUTTER AND BANANA FRENCH TOAST

This is a twist from ordinary, boring French toast. It will get your taste buds jumping with joy in the morning.

 INGREDIENTS

- 4 eggs
- 4 teaspoons vanilla
- 2 teaspoons milk
- 1 teaspoon ground cinnamon
- 8 tablespoons peanut butter
- 8 slices bread (*I love whole wheat*)
- 4 small bananas, sliced thin
- 2 tablespoons butter
- Syrup or whipped cream

 TOOLS

Knife

Whisk ·······

Measuring spoons

Small mixing bowl

Frying pan

Pancake turner/spatula

> ☼ **TIP:**
> Want to make this recipe even more fun? Use marshmallow cream instead of bananas.

#2 Bananas —Bananas have personalities! They can be mellow-yellow. They can be bold and bright. They can be just a little brown with a special sweetness. And they can always surprise you with how fresh they are under that skin of theirs. So, yes, let's get bananas on our list, especially the ones dipped in chocolate! Go bananas!

DIRECTIONS

1 **IN** a mixing bowl that is big enough for dipping slices of bread, mix the eggs, vanilla, milk, and cinnamon until well combined.

2 **SPREAD** 1 tablespoon of peanut butter on each slice of bread.

👆 **VARIATION:**
Use peanut butter and chocolate, cream cheese and jelly, or chocolate hazelnut spread for the filling.

3 **DIVIDE** the sliced bananas among four of the bread slices and top each with another slice of bread with the peanut-buttered side down.

4 **IN** the frying pan, melt the butter over a medium flame.

5 **DIP** the sandwich completely into the egg mixture; then place it in the hot butter in the frying pan.

6 **COOK** one side until brown; then flip the sandwich with a pancake turner and brown the other side.

7 **SERVE** hot with a little maple syrup, strawberry syrup, or whipped cream.

BREAKFAST FRUIT PIZZA

Who said pizza isn't for breakfast? This is a great pizza, topped with breakfast goodies.

 INGREDIENTS

- 6 cups frosted flakes, crushed
- ½ cup butter, melted
- 16 ounces cream cheese, at room temperature
- 1 jar (7 ounces) marshmallow cream
- Assortment of sliced fruit, canned or fresh

TOOLS

Mixing bowl

Measuring cups

Mixing spoon

12-inch pizza pan

Electric mixer

> 💡 **TIP:**
> These pizza slices can be refrigerated and served for a quick breakfast or an on-the-go breakfast treat.

DIRECTIONS

1 **PREHEAT** the oven to 350 degrees.

2 **STIR** together the crushed frosted flakes and melted butter. Spread and press the mixture firmly into a 12-inch pizza pan.

3 **BAKE** for 4 to 6 minutes, or until golden brown, then cool.

4 **COMBINE** the cream cheese and marshmallow cream with the mixer. Spread the mixture over the cooled crust.

5 **ARRANGE** the fruit slices to completely cover the "pizza."

6 **CUT** into wedges and serve.

Unscramble Word Game

Here you will find scrambled names of some breakfast items. Unscramble them to find popular breakfast items.

Have Fun!

FASTBREAK ____________________

NAP ____________________

OGRTYU ____________________

CESPAANK ____________________

TAOS ____________________

SLETMEO ____________________

KINGOOC RYPUS ____________________

ONCAB ____________________

KOIOCES ____________________

NOAMCNIN ____________________

HSIEGNL SIMUFNF ____________________

BRTRRSAWEY ____________________

EAMLP ____________________

SAOEGRN ____________________

EHFRNC SOTTA ____________________

Answer Key: Breakfast; Pan; Yogurt; Pancakes; Oats; Omelet; Cooking Syrup; Bacon; Cookies; Cinnamon; English Muffin; Strawberry; Maple; Oranges; French Toast

② LUNCh

Great Munches for Lunches!

W hen I was a kid, my parents would make extraspecial lunches for me. They'd make a sandwich just the way I like, or they would add something to my meal that was special, like tasty jelly cookies. Is there anything special you would like for lunch? Would you share the following section with your parents? It's about lunch and about how amazing lunchtime can be. It can help families create incredible lunchtime memories.

Mom and Dad,

If lunch is the most boring meal of the day for your kids, then this chapter is for you! Lunch can be a fun meal that provides your kids with energy to invigorate their body and mind. Think of lunch as a wonderful time to play with the colors, shapes, and flavors of your magnificent, midday meal.

If you want to know what kids really love for lunch, ask your child's schoolteacher. She has seen and heard it all. She can be your culinary spy! The lunch you pack is often discarded, as in "dumped." Think about healthy ways to entice your child to eat lunch, enjoy lunch, and to look forward to lunch. Stop taking lunch for granted, and start making brown-bag treasures that your kids will savor for their delicious possibilities!

What's for lunch? That question has been puzzling kids and adults alike for some time, and it is a question we have all heard more than once. However, have you ever thought about the question "Where *is* lunch?" The answer could be here, there, and everywhere.

The majority of lunches, especially for school-age children, are eaten outside of the home.

Packing a lunch in a special lunch box can make lunch special. Children enjoy choosing their own lunch boxes, and that privilege also will entice them to eat lunch. You can personalize this even more by photographing your child's lunch boxes over the years. You and your child will have fun doing that, and you'll enjoy the visual reminders of the ages and stages of your child's growth.

However, if you or your child prefer a brown paper bag, decorate it so that it is far from plain. Stickers and drawings can make the ordinary extraordinary!

Lunch itself does not have to be ordinary. And a packed lunch is a way to be with your kids even while you are immersed elsewhere in your daily activities. Keeping in touch this way fosters a strong bond that your child will receive with joy, and it will be long remembered. A lunch note acknowledges your concern about your child's feelings and is another way for you to express yourself. It is also a special and positive step in parent-child communication. Your message can be packed with lunch for your child as a midday pick-me-up when your child might be feeling needy, hungry, thirsty, or tired. Your note might bring a smile to your child's face during a rough day in school.

—*Chef Antonio Frontera*

Sandwiches To The Rescue

It was the fall of 1993 when the skies of Newbury Park, California, and surrounding areas became dark billowing clouds of gray. In the near distance, we could see the raging flames and other effects of the out-of-control Malibu fire. The smell became stronger, and the haze in the air increased. No one could play outside because of the awful air quality. As a teacher, I had to decide what to do with my students on those fiery days. *What was I to do?*

I sent a letter home to parents and asked them to send supplies for making lunches, although I actually was hoping I would receive magic ingredients and a solution to my dilemma. The minutes, hours, and days needed something different and unique, and my basic idea was pretty simple: we would make sandwiches and fun food, hoping that the smell of cooking would sweeten our days and that our worries about what was going on outside would be gone from our minds for a little while.

The next day was full of surprises and possibilities! Wonderful ingredients from home pantries made their way into our classroom. We had interesting discussions while we talked about quantity, equivalents, and creative cooking. We played music, and our spirits were revived by the comfort of doing something unusual at school.

Sandwiches are ideal for lunch because two pieces of bread can be the home for many a filling. Cheese, butter, meats, and brown, white, and rye breads were combined so that even the fussiest eaters were able to prepare a variety of sandwiches they liked.

Like an art project, we arranged finger sandwiches in clever combinations on cardboard platters. What might have seemed like wacky flavors became perfect creations. Some knowing family brought in a very huge sack of potatoes and a food dehydrator. That was my first time using such equipment, and it was an intriguing endeavor. We worked together, washing and peeling lots of potatoes. Next, the sliced potatoes of many sizes were placed on trays that were stacked inside the dehydrator. The slices dried and shrank to a crispy and flavorful potato chip, complete with the love put into them.

The children were excited about these "homemade" lunches, which we intended to deliver to the firefighters, who camped out at the local park between long shifts. The firefighters' faces were smudged with the ashes and smoke they encountered while fighting to save people, animals, homes, and land. Our faces were dirty and caked with food, evidence that dedicated children had prepared lunch. Parents generously volunteered to deliver the homemade sandwiches, potato chips, and other comfort foods to the busy rescue crew. Our classroom community lunch became a lunch for a community at large—a lunch of variety, flavor, fuel, and inspiration that many would long remember.

Firefighters for the catastrophe were brought in from faraway places. I used a pay phone to make a call, and next to me I heard a fireman speaking to his family saying, "I don't know exactly where this is, but I am in some town called Newbury Park." I could see the smile on his face beneath all the soot and dirt, and I heard him continue, "The people here sure are thoughtful. Even the children made us lunch." He added that the notes of gratitude and inspiration that were included with the food were like a rich dessert that made the firefighters ready to defeat the fire and save more lives.

This lunch became an act of giving, helping, and reaching out to others—and was a delicious experience!

—*Gail Small*

ANiMaL SaNDWiCheS

You can play with your food. Make the lions roar, the birds swoop through the sky, and the giraffes stretch their long, winding necks.

SERVES 2-4

INGREDiENTS

- 4 teaspoons butter
- 8 slices of bread, your choice
- 8 slices cheese, your choice
- ½ pound sliced meat, your choice

TOOLS

Big animal-shaped cookie cutters

Butter knife

Platter

DIRECTIONS

❶ SOFTEN the butter.

❷ SPREAD the butter on 2 slices of the bread.

🍴 **VARIATION:**
Fill the sandwiches with peanut butter and jelly, peanut butter and marshmallow cream, or cream cheese and jelly.

❸ PLACE 1 slice of cheese on each buttered slice.

❹ PLACE some sliced meat on top of the cheese.

❺ PLACE another slice of cheese on top of the meat, then add the other slice of bread, buttered side down.

❻ REPEAT these steps for the 3 other sandwiches.

❼ CUT off the crusts of all the sandwiches.

❽ USING metal animal-shaped cookie cutters, cut out the sandwiches.

❾ ARRANGE the sandwiches on the platter.

ENJOY YOUR TRIP TO THE ZOO!

43

ENGLISH MUFFIN Pizza

🛒 INGREDIENTS

- 4 English muffins, split
- 1 small jar (16 ounces) pizza sauce
- 8 ounces shredded mozzarella cheese

🧂 TOOLS

Spoon

Baking sheet

🍶 TIME-SAVING TIP:
You can make these ahead of time and freeze them. Defrost them as needed, and warm them up in a hurry!

SERVES 4

FUN FACT:

In 1949, Robert
O. Burton's original
prototype lunch box
was produced.

DIRECTIONS

1 **PREHEAT** the oven
to 350 degrees.

2 **LAY** out the English muffins on the
baking pan; top with the sauce
and mozzarella cheese.

3 **ADD** additional toppings
as desired.

4 **BAKE** for 15 minutes.

THINGS THAT MAKE YOU GO "HMMMM":

Did you know a tomato is actually a fruit?
In 1893, the U.S. Supreme Court ruled
to make a tomato a vegetable.

SPiLLeD MiLK

When my children were young, we walked together to the bus stop every morning. As we moved down the driveway, I mentally clicked off items from the constantly expanding checklist in my head. *Have I prepared my children well enough to go out the door on their own? Are they ready to face whatever the world throws at them?*

One morning, four-year-old Lissie and I walked my eldest child, April, to the bus stop. April was only six years old at the time, but I soon learned that she was wise beyond her years.

As usual, I was working on my checklist. My children had eaten a good breakfast. Their teeth were brushed, their faces were washed, and their hair was combed. April's milk money was tucked into an envelope in her backpack. She was wearing nice thick mittens and a handmade scarf. Still, I couldn't help wondering if she would be strong enough for the emotional, physical, and mental battles she would encounter during the course of the day. *School can be a rough place, and children can be notoriously mean.*

A small smile touched my lips as I watched my children walk down the driveway toward the bus-stop bench. Their father had made the bench and placed it a safe distance from the road. April walked with confidence, her head held high. With a backpack full of school paperwork, she looked like a young businesswoman, not a carefree first-grader. Lissie skipped beside April, zigzagging back and forth across the driveway, her attention captured a hundred times before she reached her destination.

Once they reached the bench, they both sat down to wait impatiently as I waddled toward them. They knew they were not allowed to move one step farther than the bench. They also knew that I, pregnant with their little brother, moved at a snail's pace.

When we spotted the bus, we walked the remainder of the way together. But each day, no matter how well equipped I knew April was, I worried about her welfare once she left my side. This day was no different. Will she know how to deal with a bully? *Will she know how to handle herself if she becomes ill or needs the bathroom at an inconvenient time?*

In typical, parental fashion, I kept my fears to myself and smiled reassuringly into her beautiful little face each morning before she got on the bus.

"You are going to have a wonderful day!" I proclaimed as I hugged her good-bye again.

Tipping up her face, she kissed me and hugged me back. "Bye, Mamma," she said cheerfully. April let her little sister suffocate her with a big bear hug. She giggled happily and then kissed Lissie on the nose. "Bye, Lissie."

As the bus rolled to a stop in front of us, I squatted and gave April one last hug and kiss. Lissie squeezed into my embrace, as well. Together, we whispered, "Love you like crazy!"

And then she was off.

Though Lissie and I smiled brightly, inside we were sad. Lissie continued waving long after April had disappeared. Finally, she turned to me with tear-filled eyes.

"I don't want April to go to school anymore."

> The average child will eat
> # 1,500
> peanut-butter sandwiches by high school graduation.

I bent down and hugged her. "I know. I don't either, but you know what?"

Lissie shook her head.

"April likes school. She has fun in school." I pinched Lissie's nose playfully. "And next year, you will, too!"

As soon as the bus appeared again that afternoon, Lissie and I scooted out the door. Lissie hugged April all the way back to the house. It wasn't until April took off her jacket that I noticed the chocolate-milk stains down the front of her clothes. It was as if she had taken a bath in chocolate milk!

My radar popped up immediately. I recalled another time when she had spilled her milk at the lunch table and how the children had ridiculed her. She had come home and thrown herself into my arms, sobbing as she retold the story.

I peered into her face anxiously. "Did you have an accident today?"

She shook her head. "Jimmy did."

I assumed she meant Jimmy had bumped her when she was drinking, causing her to spill her milk. "Were you okay?" I asked.

She nodded. "Jimmy spilled his milk."

I frowned. "Then how did it get on you?"

Before she could answer, Lissie raced into the room, wearing a pair of pink underpants on her head. "How do you like my crown, April? I'm the queen of Underpants Land!"

April giggled at her sister's antics. She pulled the pair of underpants off Lissie's head and yanked it over her own. While Lissie ran to get another crown, April finished her story.

"The milk spilled all over Jimmy and all over the table," she explained, peeking at me through the leg holes. "All the kids started calling him names like 'Stupid' and 'Dummy,' and they all got up and left the table. No one would sit with him."

I looked at her proudly. "But you stayed sitting by him?"

She nodded. "Uh-huh. I never said anything about the spilled milk—even when it got on me. I didn't move. I just kept eating my sandwich."

I smiled at her. "Aw, sweetie."

Her eyes grew solemn. "If I left, he wouldn't have any friends. That's what happened to me when I spilled milk that time. It made me feel bad, and I didn't want him to feel bad."

Close to tears, I looked away.

Concerned, she pressed close. "Are you okay, Mamma?" she asked, just as Lissie barreled into the room, wearing a yellow underpants crown.

I smiled. "I'm fine." I hugged April and laughed as Lissie attempted to adjust her crown so she was peeking from the leg holes, too. "I'm perfect."

As I watched my very small daughter and her even smaller sister, both wearing underpants on their heads, I knew my children—Queens of Underpants Land—really did have what it takes to make it in the world on their own.

—*Helen Kay Polaski*

Hot Dog Casserole

 Ingredients

- 1 pound rotini pasta
- 2 cups sliced hot dogs
- 1 can (32 ounces) crushed tomatoes
- 8 ounces grated mozzarella cheese
- 8 ounces grated Cheddar cheese

Tools

Serves 4-6

Pasta pot

Colander

Large mixing bowl

Knife

Mixing spoon

Large casserole dish

Grater

DiRECTiONS

1 PREhEaT the oven to 350 degrees.

2 COOK the pasta by following the package instructions, drain it in the colander, and place it in the large mixing bowl.

3 SLiCE the hot dogs into ½-inch pieces and add them to the cooked pasta. Add the tomatoes and cheeses and toss to combine.

4 PuT the mixture in the casserole dish; then bake for 30 to 35 minutes.

TIP:
Coat your grater with nonstick spray before using it. It will be much easier to clean up.

Doggy Bean Bake

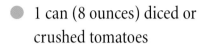

🛒 INGREDIENTS

- 1 pound hot dogs, cut into quarters
- 1 can (32 ounces) pork and beans
- 1 can (8 ounces) diced or crushed tomatoes
- 1 tablespoon Dijon mustard
- 1 tablespoon sugar
- 1 egg
- 2 ⅔ cups milk
- ¼ cup oil
- ½ cup corn kernels
- 1 ½ teaspoons baking powder
- ¾ cup all-purpose flour

🍴 TOOLS

2 mixing bowls

Measuring spoons

Measuring cups

Mixing spoon

Large casserole dish

Toothpick

SERVES 5–6

DIRECTIONS

1 PREHEAT the oven to 375 degrees.

2 COMBINE the hot dogs, beans, tomatoes, and mustard in a mixing bowl.

3 IN the other mixing bowl, mix the sugar, egg, milk, oil, corn, baking powder, and flour. Stir until smooth.

4 PUT the hot dog mixture into the casserole dish.

5 SPOON the milk mixture over the hot dog mixture. Smooth the topping as much as you can.

6 BAKE 35 to 40 minutes until golden brown and a toothpick inserted in the center comes out clean.

CHILDREN GRIEVE, TOO

When my dad died after a long battle with cancer, my three young children were devastated at losing their beloved grandpa. But they were also fascinated and puzzled at the ritual of people bringing food to our bereaved family. I explained that friends and neighbors cook for people who are sad to show that they love them.

As streams of people continued to arrive, bearing tuna casseroles and meatloaf, broccoli and green beans, coconut cakes and brownies with nuts, my six-year-old daughter climbed onto my lap and put her arms around my neck.

"Don't any of these people love us kids, Mama?" she asked, her eyes brimming with tears.

"Of course they do, sweetheart. Why would you ask such a thing?"

"Because we don't like tuna casserole or broccoli or coconut cake. And we hate nuts in our brownies!"

"What do you wish they had brought?"

"Macaroni and cheese and hot dogs. Brownies with no nuts."

I hugged her tight. "I guess sometimes grown-ups just forget about what children like to eat. But you know what? It's something we're going to try to remember."

And we have. Over the years, as friends and neighbors have experienced deaths in their own families, my children have insisted that we cook "kid food" if there are children among the bereaved. We never have to discuss what casserole or dessert we'll prepare and take to them. We keep the ingredients on hand. And when the thank-you notes arrive, they invariably say, *Thank you for thinking of the children during this difficult time. They loved what you cooked.*

—*Jennie Ivey*

HOT DOGS WITH CHEESE

A hot dog walks into a bookstore and asks for a soda.

The shopkeeper replies, "Sorry, we don't serve food here."

That joke is pretty cheesy—just like these dogs!

 INGREDIENTS

- 6 hot dogs
- 6 to 8 ounces shredded Cheddar cheese

TOOLS

Knife

Baking sheet pan

💡 TIP: Frozen cheese is easier to grate.

DIRECTIONS

1 PREHEAT the oven to 400 degrees.

2 MAKE a lengthwise slit halfway into the hot dogs.

SERVES 3-4

3 STUFF cheese into each slit.

4 PLACE the stuffed hot dogs on the baking sheet.

5 BAKE until the hot dog is cooked and the cheese is melted.

The Ultimate Mac-'N-Cheese

Serves 4-6

Mac-n-cheese is comfort to your soul and your mind, and of course, your family.

—Chef Antonio Frontera

Ingredients

- 2 pounds macaroni (shells are good)
- Cheddar cheese sauce (4 ounces) *(Most commonly used is Velvetta cheese.)*
- 4 ounces shredded Cheddar cheese
- 4 ounces shredded provolone
- 4 ounces shredded mozzarella
- ½ pound (2 sticks) butter
- 2 cups milk
- 1 cup half-and-half
- 1 cup seasoned bread crumbs

Tools

Pasta pot

Colander

Measuring cup

Mixing spoon

Large rectangular baking pan

Ooey, gooey, cheesy, yum, yum!

DiReCTioNS

1 **PREhEaT** the oven to 350 degrees.

2 **BoiL** the macaroni until cooked.

3 **DRaiN** the macaroni.
Put it back in the pasta pot
and add the Cheddar cheese
sauce and the provolone,
mozzarella, butter, milk, and
half-and-half. Stir the mixture
on low heat until blended.

4 **PoUR** the mixture into the large rectangular baking pan.
Sprinkle the bread crumbs over the mixture to cover it
completely.

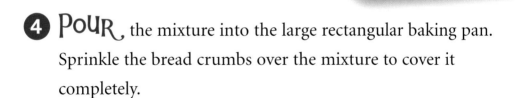

> **🍎 HEALTHY TIP:**
> Use part-skim for all
> of the cheese and use
> whole wheat pasta
> instead of white.

5 **SPRiNKLE** the shredded
Cheddar cheese on top and bake the
mac-'n-cheese for 15 to 20 minutes.
Take it out of the oven; let it sit for
10 minutes and serve.

COOKING OUTDOORS

O n my first day at Blue Bird Camp, the counselor told us we would cook our lunch over a fire. We were not going to use pans. I was curious. *How do you cook without pans?* I'd had marshmallows cooked on a stick over a fire, but marshmallows weren't a real meal. The counselor promised, "This will be the best lunch you ever ate."

We hiked through the woods, stepping on stones to cross a small brook and listening to birds and squirrels. One of the girls caught a lizard. The counselor wore a red backpack, and our mystery lunch was in there. All of us girls kept asking, "What's for lunch?" The counselor just smiled and said, "You'll love it."

Finally, we came to a blackened stone ring where the counselor took off her backpack and sent us to gather sticks. Soon we had a roaring fire, and the counselor passed out potato slices and pieces of aluminum foil. Our counselor opened a huge can of tuna fish. We each ladled some of that onto our potatoes. We topped the tuna and potatoes with tomato slices. Then we crinkled up our aluminum foil, using it to cover the potato, tuna, and tomato. Finally, we took turns using a huge pair of tongs to put our aluminum foil bundles into the fire.

While our lunches cooked, the counselor let each of us take a glob of bread dough and work it onto the end of a long stick. There was a collection of these sticks by the fire pit, obviously used by earlier campers. Then we cooked our bread marshmallow style over the fire and sang camping songs while our tuna-potato mixtures cooked.

When the bread was cooked, we waited for it to cool a little before pulling it off the stick. The counselor came around and put a glob of butter into the holes in the bread where the sticks had been. We tilted our dough around, watching the butter melt as it coated the bread. I'd never had fresh bread before—it was fantastic, all warm and steaming.

The counselor passed out carrot sticks and celery sticks. We ate them impatiently, waiting for the mystery meal cooking in the fire. I remember imagining that the potatoes, tuna, and tomatoes would magically transform themselves into something exciting, while they hid in their wrapped packets in the fire. Finally, the counselor said our aluminum foil packets were done. She pulled them out of the fire.

I was impatient as I waited for the packet to cool enough to open it. The counselor finally cut our packets open with the tines of a big fork. I was filled with expectation. Steam gushed out with a sweet, tomato aroma. But when I looked into it, my packet still contained just potatoes, canned tuna, and softened tomato slices. The only real difference was that our food was now hot.

I used my plastic fork and took a taste gingerly. Potatoes, tuna, and cooked tomato slices. I liked it. And I was a picky eater. There is something about cooking over a fire that makes the most ordinary food special— maybe even a bit magical.

—*Lois June Wickstrom*

HaMBURGER BaKED BEaNS

🛒 INGREDIENTS

- 4 slices bacon
- 1 pound ground beef
- 1 medium onion, peeled and chopped
- 1½ teaspoons salt
- 2 cans (16 ounces each) pork and beans
- ½ cup ketchup
- ½ cup brown sugar
- 1 teaspoon Dijon mustard

SERVES 6-8

🍴 TOOLS

Microwave or frying pan

Saucepan

Mixing bowl

Mixing spoon

Measuring spoons

Measuring cups

Large casserole dish

> 🥄 **TIME-SAVING TIP:**
> If you're in a rush,
> this casserole can be made
> in a saucepan on the stove
> and placed on a bun.

DIRECTIONS

1 **PREHEAT** the oven to 350 degrees.

2 **COOK.** the bacon until crispy in the microwave or frying pan, then crumble it.

3 **IN** the saucepan, brown the ground beef and add the onion. Drain the excess fat; then spread the beef and onion mixture evenly in the large casserole dish.

4 **SPRINKLE** the bacon on the ground beef.

5 **COMBINE** the salt, pork and beans, ketchup, brown sugar, and mustard in the mixing bowl, then pour the mixture on top of the bacon.

6 **BAKE** for 60 to 75 minutes until hot and bubbly.

DELICATE FOOD

"Look, I made you an egg with your name written on it," my younger sister said, greeting me at the door and juggling a decorated egg.

"Sure enough, and you dipped it in purple, my favorite color." I set down a grocery bag so I could give Lori my full attention. My name, written in crayon, circled the egg and ended with an exclamation mark.

Mother and Lori had boiled eggs the previous night in preparation for today. Now the smell of vinegar permeated the house, and my sister's hands showed traces of experimentation with color.

This morning Mother had agreed to let me drive on the holiday errand run. With company coming, I knew she could use help gathering food and flowers. We had dropped my brother, David, at the local park for his soccer practice, and he had assured us he would get a ride home later.

My mother had called out instructions to him as we pulled away. "Come home right after practice. Your grandparents are coming, and I want you to be clean." My brother waved. David, his blond hair glowing in the sun, has the same wave as my father. I had recognized the tilt of his head and the bemused grin that had complemented the casual swish of his hand. Dad had used the same wave this morning, when we had left on the errand run. My father had reassured us that he and Lori would have fun decorating eggs and would leave minimal mess.

Indeed, other than Lori's hands and a smudge of red on her cheek, the kitchen was clean. My mother entered with her load, and we began to unpack the groceries. David arrived home and pawed through the bags, hoping for a quick snack. My mother sent him to the shower. She promised us that lunch would be ready by the time my grandparents arrived.

My mother picked up several of Lori's decorated eggs. Suddenly, she looked puzzled. "Steve? Would you come here, please?" My mother's voice had a high-pitched tone. My dad came into the kitchen with my grandparents trailing happily behind him.

"Look who I found at the front door. They were about to ring the bell." My father was beaming but oblivious and blindsided by my mother's next question.

"Steve, what eggs did you use this morning?"

Then Lori piped up. "The ones on the middle shelf that we boiled last night." My father looked from her to my mother to see if this was a good answer.

Mother burst into laughter and shook her head. "How in the world did you two manage not to break a single egg?" She pointed to the egg carton in her hands. "*These* are the hard-boiled eggs. You grabbed the wrong cartons. I know exactly what happened. I rearranged the fridge this morning before I finalized my grocery list. Lori, honey, your beautiful colored eggs are raw, and we need to get them in the fridge!"

Lori's eyes brimmed with tears as she realized that her art was being recalled from the display shelf.

My grandmother said, "It's been a long time since I've decorated eggs."

My kindly, rumpled grandfather got out his car keys. He spoke to Lori. "What if I get us another dye kit? After lunch, we'll color all the eggs your mother tried to hide from you."

Mother and Dad nodded. Lori smiled gleefully, all tears forgotten, and David came into the kitchen still toweling his hair. "What's going on? Did I miss lunch?"

My grandmother grabbed him in a bear hug. "Grandson, I hope you worked up an appetite for scrambled and hard-boiled eggs. I bet that's the menu for the next week."

—*Joanne L. Faries*

Egg Salad

SERVES
3–4

Each year, 87 billion chicken eggs are produced in the United States. The average person eats the equivalent of 254 eggs annually. And now, here go 10 more!

 ## INGREDIENTS

- 10 eggs
- ¾ cup mayonnaise
- 3 tablespoons Dijon mustard
- ½ teaspoon celery seeds
- Salt and pepper

 ## TOOLS

Saucepan

Mixing bowl

Knife

Mixing spoon

Measuring cups

Measuring spoons

DIRECTIONS

1 BOIL the eggs in the saucepan and then remove the shells.

2 CHOP the eggs and put them in the mixing bowl. Add the mayonnaise, mustard, celery seeds, and salt and pepper to taste. Mix everything thoroughly.

> 💡 **TIP:**
> For quicker, easier peeling, place eggs in ice water after they are cooked.

Snow and Soup

My mother placed a pot of chicken broth on the stove. After a while, she plucked a few leaves of thyme from a plant on the windowsill. The thyme's wonderful, earthy smell filled the room. She tossed the thyme into the pot, and then she threw in two fistfuls of spiky noodles.

My mother took a break from cooking and looked out the kitchen window, hands on her hips. She saw my friends and me standing in three feet of snow, arguing.

It was really cold, and Robert's breath came out in plumes of vapor. He sheathed his numb, red hands in gloves and wailed, "Come on, guys, let me back into the game!"

Jim glared at Robert. "But you're out! We hit you with snowballs ten times. You know the rules. You're out."

"But that's not fair! I only got to play for five minutes. And the game just started!"

"Tough. You know the rules."

I watched Robert's face. The frown on his lips began to quiver, as if he were going to cry. His eyes widened, and his eyebrows drooped. Robert looked really upset, and I felt sorry for him. But I usually felt bad for him. For the most part, he was kind of a loner, and most kids generally avoided him.

I said, "Come on, guys. Who cares about the rules? Let Robert back into the game."

Inside the house, my mother, who couldn't hear what we were saying, frowned and returned to cooking. She chopped up chives. The green, spicy smell of the chives mingled with the earthy smell of the thyme. My mother tossed the chives into the pot. Then she left the stove for a moment. She took a bag of leftover chicken out of the refrigerator and placed it on the counter. She returned to the stove and began to stir the soup with a well-worn wooden spoon.

Outside, all my friends were getting pretty stirred up. Jim looked angry. He turned and spoke harshly to me. "Andrew, you know the rules. Robert is out. That's the way the game is!"

Another friend, Jason, jumped into the conversation. "He's out. That's it. Come on, let's get back to playing."

I responded, "This game is supposed to be fun. We're *all* supposed to have fun. Let Robert play!"

Robert stopped quivering. He looked relieved. Someone was standing up for him. Robert said, "Yeah. And we just started playing. I don't want to be out. I don't want to sit and watch the rest of you play for hours!"

Jason, exasperated, agreed. "Sure. Okay. Whatever." Some of my friends mumbled beneath their breath, but Robert was allowed back in the game.

Inside the house, my mother resumed stirring the soup. She took the bag of chicken from the counter and opened it. She took the chicken out of the bag and put it into the pot. Then she stirred the soup. The broth was hot enough that bubbles were jumping all around, dancing wildly.

The game outside was raging. Snowballs were flying, and my friends were yelling, "You're hit."

"Ha ha! You missed me!"

"I'll bet I can get you with the next one."

I didn't notice Robert creeping up behind me. Suddenly, he started pelting me with snowballs. He threw the snowballs too hard. It wasn't a game for him—it was war—and the snowballs stung my skin. I started to yell, "You're throwing them too . . ."

I couldn't finish my sentence because a snowball struck my mouth, burning my lips. Robert was almost on top of me, and he was still throwing snowballs at me. The balls punched at my skin, and snow got caked in my ears and hair. "Stop. That's it. STOP!" I shrieked.

Robert's war ended. He finished throwing snowballs and yelled, "You're out!"

I was really angry. I opened my mouth to yell at Robert, but then I realized something. I'd never seen Robert so happy before. He was laughing, and he looked triumphant. For the first time since I'd met him, he looked confident and proud of himself. I decided not to fight. Why ruin the moment for him? Fighting would do neither of us any good.

"Okay," I said, "I'm out. Robert, when you get a chance, tell the rest of the guys that I'm done for the day. Okay? Tell them that I went in for dinner. By the way, Robert, that was pretty good. You're great at this game. You know that? Wow!"

Robert beamed at the compliment. His smile broadened, and he laughed.

I walked into my house and pulled off my snow clothes. I pulled chunks of snow from my hair and scraped ice off the front of my turtleneck.

When I entered the kitchen, my mother saw how ragged I looked. She brought me over to the stove, put my small, cold hand in her warm one, and let me stir the soup. The soup's swirling steam warmed my face, and the delightful kitchen smells relaxed me. My mom stood behind me, handed me a shaker, and let me add pepper to the soup.

A little later, we ate, and it was delicious. Yeah, it hurt a little, helping Robert to feel good about himself. But the pain was nothing that chicken noodle soup couldn't fix. The chicken soup made me feel warm and wonderful. Something so simple can make you feel so good.

—*Andrew J. Corsa*

ChicKeN SouP FOR The SouL

 INGREDIENTS

- 1 onion, peeled
- 1 carrot
- 2 stalks celery
- 1 potato
- 6 cups chicken broth (canned or homemade, recipe follows)
- 6 ounces uncooked noodles
- 1½ cups cooked and shredded chicken

TOOLS

Knife

Cutting board

Soup pot

TIME-SAVING TIP:
Use a bag or box of frozen mixed vegetables.

HERE you haVE The ULTIMATE ChiCKEN SouP!

DiReCTioNS

1 **Wash** and chop the onion, carrot, celery, and potato into small pieces. Add the broth and simmer until all vegetables are tender, approximately 8 minutes, depending on the size of the vegetable pieces.

2 **ADD** the noodles to the broth and cook them until tender, or approximately 8 to 10 minutes. Add the chicken and simmer for another 2 minutes until the chicken is heated all the way through.

#3 ChiCKEN SouP—The best food is golden, warm, and smooth. You can have it with noodles, with crackers, and even with little chunks of bread. You can eat it from a bowl or drink it from a cup. Any way, it tastes like a hug. It's chicken soup, and everybody loves it because it warms your tummy—and your heart.

Chicken Broth

🛒 Ingredients

- 4 pounds whole chicken or chicken pieces, including necks and backs
- 2 large onions, peeled
- 4 carrots
- 4 pieces celery, including leaves
- 2 cloves garlic
- 1 zucchini
- 1 potato, peeled
- 3 bay leaves
- 8 quarts (32 cups) water

🏺 Tools

Knife

Cutting board

Stockpot

Ladle or skimmer

Container (or another stockpot)

> ☼ **TIP:**
> You can refrigerate this broth for up to 5 days and can use it for many dishes, or you can freeze it in portions that you can defrost as needed.

FUN GAME:
Add a bay leaf to one of the bowls, prior to serving the soup. Whoever gets it wins a prize!

DIRECTIONS

MAKES
1½
GALLONS

1 **Wash** carrots, celery, zucchini, and potato, and cut each of these and the garlic and onion into 4 pieces.

2 **PUT** the chicken, the vegetables, and the bay leaves into the stockpot, then add the water. Bring the mixture to a boil on high heat, then lower it to medium heat.

3 **SIMMER** the stock for 6 to 7 hours. Periodically skim the fat and foam off the top with the ladle or skimmer.

4 **WHEN** the soup tastes the way you like it, drain it through a colander into another container. (You can cut up the cooked chicken for the soup, but throw everything else away.) Now you have the chicken stock ready for your Chicken Soup for the Soul.

KnickKnacks

Mrs. Wilson invited all the little girls from our church for a tea party. This was so exciting because it was the first time I had ever been invited to an adult's house. I remember feeling so important and privileged to be attending. After all, Mrs. Wilson was one of the dearest people in our church, and she always treated me like a little lady by asking me how I was doing, or giving me a compliment on my Sunday dress.

My mom explained that Mrs. Wilson was in her seventies and that her children were grown. I was shocked to find out that she had been my dad's language teacher when he was a boy. He told me that she had been his favorite teacher, so I made sure to look extra nice for the special event that I was wholeheartedly dying to attend.

The other five girls and I arrived at just about the same time. Mrs. Wilson's home was just as I expected it: a cozy, sun-filled cottage fit for a queen. She greeted each one of us and thanked us for coming to visit with her. A tea set, a plate of tiny finger sandwiches made with crust-free bread, and many different types of fresh baked goodies were placed neatly atop a lace tablecloth. Mrs. Wilson wasn't quite finished preparing her most memorable salad when we arrived, so she asked us if we wanted to help her. Of course we all agreed eagerly.

Although she only allowed us to mix in the fruit and nuts as she did the rest, I felt very ladylike to be helping Mrs. Wilson in her kitchen and appreciated every minute of it. The creamy Waldorf salad tasted magical to me. I was probably the only little girl to ask for seconds. As you can

READER/CUSTOMER CARE SURVEY

CGGG

We care about your opinions! Please take a moment to fill out our online Reader Survey at **http://survey.hcibooks.com**. As a **"THANK YOU"** you will receive a **VALUABLE INSTANT COUPON** towards future book purchases as well as a **SPECIAL GIFT** available only online! Or, you may mail this card back to us and we will send you a copy of our exciting catalog with your valuable coupon inside.

First Name _____ MI. ____ Last Name _____

Address _____

State _____ Zip _____ Email _____ City _____

1. Gender
❑ Female ❑ Male

2. Age
❑ 8 or younger
❑ 9-12 ❑ 13-16
❑ 17-20 ❑ 21-30
❑ 31+

3. Did you receive this book as a gift?
❑ Yes ❑ No

4. Annual Household Income
❑ under $25,000
❑ $25,000 - $34,999
❑ $35,000 - $49,999
❑ $50,000 - $74,999
❑ over $75,000

5. What are the ages of the children living in your house?
❑ 0 - 14
❑ 15+

6. Marital Status
❑ Single ❑ Married
❑ Divorced ❑ Widowed

7. How did you find out about the book?
(please choose one)
❑ Recommendation
❑ Store Display
❑ Online
❑ Catalog/Mailing
❑ Interview/Review

8. Where do you usually buy books?
(please choose one)
❑ Bookstore
❑ Online
❑ Book Club/Mail Order
❑ Price Club (Sam's Club, Costco's, etc.)
❑ Retail Store (Target, Wal-Mart, etc.)

9. What subject do you enjoy reading about the most?
(please choose one)
❑ Parenting/Family
❑ Relationships
❑ Recovery/Addictions
❑ Health/Nutrition
❑ Christianity
❑ Spirituality/Inspiration
❑ Business Self-help
❑ Women's Issues
❑ Sports

10. What attracts you most to a book?
(please choose one)
❑ Title
❑ Cover Design
❑ Author
❑ Content

TAPE IN MIDDLE; DO NOT STAPLE

BUSINESS REPLY MAIL
FIRST-CLASS MAIL PERMIT NO 45 DEERFIELD BEACH, FL

POSTAGE WILL BE PAID BY ADDRESSEE

Chicken Soup for the Soul Kids in the Kitchen
3201 SW 15th Street
Deerfield Beach, FL 33442-9875

FOLD HERE

Do you have your own Chicken Soup story
that you would like to send us?
Please submit at: **www.chickensoup.com**

Comments

imagine, the others were primarily interested in the cookies and baked goods.

Mrs. Wilson played a couple of songs for us on her piano, and we sang along to a few Sunday school hymns. I'm certain it was a great day for all of the girls, but for me that day will always remain in a special place in my heart.

Before we bid farewell, Mrs. Wilson allowed each of us to pick out one of the knickknacks from her cabinet. In my careful decision to choose just the right one, I finally decided on a small blue porcelain basket, which reminded me of Mrs. Wilson's blue Waldorf salad bowls. Beaming a smile from ear to ear, she gave us all a gentle wave good-bye and said she would see us again soon.

I'm not sure who has moved into her cozy cottage, or if they know that a beautiful soul once lived there, but Mrs. Wilson now lives in a palace fit for a queen with her heavenly Father. I still have that little porcelain basket, and each time I look at it, I remember that smile and the lesson she taught me: "All it takes is a smile and a little helping hand."

—*Amy Luciano*

MRS. WILSON'S WALDORF SALAD

We all have our favorites! Although Mrs. Wilson made this salad very well, you also can make it—and it will be just as delicious.

INGREDIENTS

- 2 cups coarsely chopped apples
- ½ cup chopped celery
- ½ cup grated carrots
- ½ cup mayonnaise
- ⅓ cup chopped walnuts
- ⅓ cup raisins
- ¼ teaspoon lemon juice

TOOLS

Knife

Cutting board

Mixing bowl

Measuring cups

Measuring spoons

Mixing spoon

Grater

 VARIATION:
Make this a full meal by adding some cut-up, cooked chicken to this delicious salad.

DIRECTIONS

1 **Mix** apples, celery, carrots, mayonnaise, walnuts, raisins, and lemon juice in the mixing bowl.

2 **Chill** in the refrigerator for 1 hour and serve.

SERVES
4

Delicious!

The Legacy of Pizza Crackers

Dad was the rainbow after the storm, the sunshine through the clouds, and the pillar of strength for the discouraged. He was six feet tall and very handsome. In my eyes, he was a heartthrob full of zeal and energy. He squeezed every ounce out of life. We would roast marshmallows in the fireplace, play croquet in the backyard, and have watergun fights on hot summer days. The funnest place in the world to be was at my house.

My father was many things, but the one thing he was not was a cook. A frozen pizza would present itself as a challenge to my father.

However, after one exhausting high-pressure day in second grade, I came home to find Dad perky in the kitchen.

"Hey, kiddo," he said, "are you hungry?"

I scanned the counters to find that there was no takeout pizza, and I didn't see any sandwich meat. *Perhaps he was going to offer to buy me Burger King.*

"Yeah, I'm pretty hungry!" I replied.

"Good, then I have the perfect meal for you. You are going to love what I am going to make."

Experimental cooking: the thought of dad making anything caused my stomach to churn. *What had I gotten myself into?*

Dad pulled out a jar of pizza sauce, a box of crackers, mozzarella cheese, and some pepperoni slices. He began to hum and dance around the kitchen.

76

I saw most of the ingredients for pizza, *but what did he need with crackers?* My curiosity was getting the best of me.

"Well, Squirt, would you like to help? I am going to make my world-famous pizza crackers."

"Slap some of this pizza sauce on the crackers."

After that, we sprinkled the crackers with mozzarella cheese and placed pepperoni on top of that.

Then Dad said, "Now put them in the microwave for thirty seconds."

The delicious smell that filled the kitchen was invigorating. My stomach rumbled at the thought of being fed.

Dad pulled the pizza crackers out of the microwave and said, "Before you try one, you have to do the pizza-cracker dance with me."

I held on to the back of his waist, and we danced around the kitchen chanting, "Pizza crackers, what a nifty treat—just some pizza on a cracker, but a lot of fun to eat!"

I loved Dad's amazing invention. We made more than pizza crackers that day; we made a memory so amazing that I want the legacy to live on with my children and grandchildren.

—*Jennifer Smith*

Pizza Crackers

🛒 Ingredients

- 1 jar (26 ounces) pizza sauce (or your homemade favorite)
- 1 box (8 ounces) round crackers
- 1 package (8 ounces) sliced pepperoni
- 8 ounces shredded mozzarella cheese

🥄 Tools

Spreading knife

Cookie sheet or pizza pan

Pancake turner or spatula

This recipe is easy as pie!

DIRECTIONS

1 **PREHEAT** the oven to 350 degrees.

2 **SPREAD** the pizza sauce on the crackers.

3 **PLACE** the sliced pepperoni on the sauce.

4 **SPRINKLE** with the mozzarella cheese.

5 **PLACE** the pizza crackers on the baking pan and bake for 5 to 10 minutes.

6 **TAKE** the pan out of the oven, remove the pizza crackers with the pancake turner, and eat.

TIME-SAVING TIP:
If you're in a hurry, place the crackers in a microwave for 30 seconds and—like magic—they're done!

SERVES
10–12

Skinny Pigs in a Blanket

🛒 INGREDIENTS

- 10 slices whole wheat bread
- 6 tablespoons mustard
- 10 turkey hot dogs
- Seasoned nonstick cooking spray

SERVES 10

🧰 TOOLS

Measuring spoon

Small spatula or butter knife

Cookie sheet pan

D on't eat like a pig. Recent studies show that nearly 63 percent of Americans are obese. So when you eat a pig, make sure it's skinny!

DIRECTIONS

1 **PREHEAT** the oven to 375 degrees.

2 **LAY** out the slices of bread on a counter or table. Spread the mustard on the bread.

3 **PLACE** 1 hot dog on each slice of bread, then roll up the bread to enclose the hot dog, with the seam side down.

4 **APPLY** the nonstick cooking spray to the cookie sheet pan and place the "pigs in a blanket" seam down on the pan.

5 **BAKE** for 15 to 20 minutes, or until golden brown.

Whole-Wheat Wraps

W hen you're wrapped up in errands, and have no time, wrap these up and enjoy a fast, easy treat—maybe with a cup of tea!

Serves 8

🛒 **Ingredients**

- 4 8-inch whole-wheat tortillas
- ¼ cup peanut butter
- 4 bananas
- 4 teaspoons honey
- 4 tablespoons granola

🏺 **Tools**

Small spatula

Knife

Measuring cup

Measuring spoons

DIRECTIONS

1 **Lay** the tortillas out on a counter or table.

2 **SPREAD** the peanut butter evenly on the tortillas, leaving ¼ inch uncovered all the way around the edges.

3 **CUT** the bananas in half lengthwise; place 2 pieces on each tortilla.

4 **DRIZZLE** 1 teaspoon of honey on each banana, then sprinkle with 1 tablespoon of the granola.

5 **FOLD** in the sides, roll up, and seal. Cut in half. Serve seam side down.

CHICKEN NUGGETS

INGREDIENTS

- 1 whole chicken breast, skinned and deboned
- 1 cup whole-wheat bread crumbs
- ½ teaspoon garlic powder
- ¼ teaspoon black pepper
- ¼ teaspoon salt
- 1 egg white
- 1 tablespoon water
- Lowfat cooking spray

TOOLS

Stainless steel mixing bowl

Another mixing bowl

Shallow baking pan

Measuring spoon

Measuring cup

Mixing spoon

Baking pan

Knife

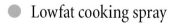

Directions

1 **PREHEAT** the oven to 350 degrees.

2 **CUT** the chicken into 1-inch cubes.

3 **IN** the stainless steel mixing bowl, combine the bread crumbs, garlic powder, black pepper, and salt.

4 **IN** the other bowl, mix together the egg white and water.

5 **SPRAY** the baking pan with the lowfat cooking spray.

6 **DIP** the chicken into the egg-water mixture and then into the bread crumb mixture until the cubes are completely coated. Then place the nuggets on the prepared pan.

7 **SPRAY** the nuggets with some more lowfat cooking spray.

8 **BAKE** for 15 to 20 minutes or until chicken is cooked all the way through and golden brown.

Lunch Matching Game

You don't want to be caught without lunch! Match up the words on the left to the ones on the right to make a great lunch item!

Peanut Butter	Tuna
Egg	Wrap
English Muffin	Salad
Hot Dog	Patty
Macaroni	Lettuce, Tomato
Pizza	Burrito
Chicken	Jelly
Hamburger	Cheese
Swiss Cheese	Beans
Salad	Cream Cheese
Jelly	Pizza
Beef	Crackers
Bean	Soup
Bacon	French Fries
Turkey	Ham

3 DiNNER

What's for Dinner?

*W*hat's for dinner? I bet you have asked that question a million times. Well, it's all about memories—dinner memories, that is.

In this chapter, you will find different types of food from various countries. The key here is to cook a nice dinner and eat together. You may want to play some food games, like put a bay leaf in a bowl of soup, and whomever gets it, gets a special something—whether it's an extra serving, or an extra thirty minutes of TV, or not having to wash the dishes.

But you know what? I realize it wasn't all that bad when I washed the dishes and my mom and dad dried them. It was the perfect time to have a heart-to-heart talk. You may not realize it now, but eating together and cleaning up afterward will provide some of the best memories of your early years, so go ahead and experiment. Have fun, grab that whisk or that pot and pan, and use it, then gather around the dining room table and enjoy yourselves. There are no rules for dinner memories.

—*Chef Antonio Frontera*

Sharing The Dough

"I like helping you cook, Mom," Katrina chirped.

She whacked the tube of crescent rolls against the edge of the kitchen counter. When it popped open, she peeled away the wrapper and pulled out the yeasty-smelling dough. "Mmmmm. This smells good."

"Don't pull them all apart. It says to separate them into rectangles instead of triangles," I read from the recipe card. "Do you remember what rectangles are?"

Five-year-old Katrina nodded. Gently pulling at the serrated edges, she laid the rectangles side by side until she filled the casserole pan. "But they don't fit," she pointed out. "I can see the bottom of the pan."

"Use your fingertips and press the edges together," I demonstrated. While she finished, I got out the hand mixer and a bowl. "Would you like to beat the eggs?"

It wasn't long before we'd added all the ingredients to make that night's supper: Crescent Pizza, a dish our family loved. As it baked in the oven, Katrina and I cleared the counter and got out plates to set the kitchen table.

Katrina's tummy rumbled loudly. "I'm hungry, Mom!"

"Call everyone to the table, then. The oven timer will go off any minute."

Rrrrrrring.

Wiping my hands on a yellow terry towel, I reached for the phone.

"Hello?" I listened intently as our bishop's wife explained a problem she needed my help with. "Why, of course we can do that. Dinner is almost ready, so we'll be right there."

I turned to see that everyone had filed into the kitchen. "The church discovered a family living out of its car—no home, no money, nothing to eat." I turned to the kids and asked, "What would you think about giving them our supper?"

The kids eyed each other uncertainly. No one said a word. When Katrina's stomach rumbled again in protest, she placed her palm flat against it and looked up. "Our *whole* supper?"

"Well, yes. It's done. It's hot. It's nutritious. And the family is hungry."

"So am *I*," Katrina whined as I bent over the open oven door and pulled out the bubbling pizza.

"Are you?" My brows lifted and my forehead wrinkled. "Honestly?"

Katrina stared at the steaming pan I'd set on the counter. She breathed in the warm scent of hot bread and baked ham. She listened to her grumbling stomach.

"These people *really* don't have any money?"

I could hear the doubt in her voice. "None," I said.

"And no home at all?" Her lower lip trembled.

"No home." I decided to press my point. "And no nice, warm kitchen with a loaded refrigerator and pantry full of food."

"Then I guess we'd better take them some supper." She paused for a long moment. "Mom, is there time to make dessert? I bet they'd like some pudding, too."

"I bet they would," I agreed. "What flavor would you suggest?"

"Chocolate," she said. "And, can we add banana slices? That's my favorite!"

I nodded, proud of her decision to share a tasty dish, to bring pleasure and comfort and satisfaction to others, and to warm and fill empty stomachs. Already she was learning the ingredients necessary to become a good cook.

After all, I smiled, *the proof was in the pudding.*

—*Carol McAdoo Rehme*

Cooking is easy. You put some stuff on the stove, burn it and then order pizza. My mom does it all the time.

CRESCENT Pizza

INGREDIENTS

- 2 cups cubed ham
- 1 tablespoon onion powder
- 1 package (8 ounces) crescent rolls
- 4 eggs
- ¼ teaspoon black pepper
- ½ cup milk
- 1 cup shredded Cheddar cheese
- ¼ cup sliced black olives

TOOLS

Large rectangular baking pan

Mixing bowl

Whisk

Measuring spoons

Measuring cups

SERVES 6–8

FUN FACT:
Americans eat approximately 350 slices of pizza per second.

Directions

1 **Preheat** the oven to 375 degrees.

2 **Season** the ham with the onion powder.

3 **Pat** the crescent roll dough into the large rectangular baking pan and press it to cover the pan bottom and ½ inch up the sides. Sprinkle the ham over the dough.

4 **Beat** together the eggs, pepper, milk, and cheese. Pour this over the ham mixture.

5 **Sprinkle** the black olives over the top of the mixture.

6 **Bake** for 25 to 30 minutes until golden brown.

TURKEY CHILI

W ho said chili was only for beef?
Enjoy this on a cold winter night.

SERVES
4

INGREDIENTS

- 1 small onion, peeled
- 1 small green bell pepper, seeds removed
- 1 red bell pepper, seeds removed
- 1 tablespoon olive oil
- ½ pound ground turkey meat
- 1 can (16 ounces) tomato sauce or crushed tomatoes
- 1 can (14 ounces) red kidney beans
- ½ teaspoon oregano
- 1½ teaspoons chili powder
- ¼ teaspoon Cajun spice

TOOLS

Small bowl

Cutting board

Saucepan with lid

Measuring spoons

Mixing spoon

Can opener

Knife

VARIATION:
Add some cooked, cut-up sweet potatoes, or use beef instead of turkey.

Directions

1 **Chop** the onions and green and red peppers into small pieces; set them aside in the bowl.

2 **Heat** the oil in the saucepan over medium heat. Then cook the ground turkey until browned. Drain any excess oil and return the turkey to the saucepan.

3 **ADD** the chopped onion and peppers and stir.

4 **ADD** the tomatoes, beans, oregano, chili powder, and Cajun spice and stir.

5 **Bring** to a simmer, then cover and simmer on low heat for 20 minutes.

☼ SERVING TIP:
Serve over cornbread for a meal in one!

1-2-3 Beef Stew

Enjoy this stew on a cool winter night.

INGREDIENTS

- ½ pound white mushrooms
- 1 pound leftover roast beef
- 2 cups beef broth
- 2 cups canned brown gravy
- 1½ cups frozen peas and carrots mix
- 1 bay leaf
- 1 package egg noodles

TOOLS

Knife

Measuring cups

Saucepan

Mixing spoon

DIRECTIONS

1 **REMOVE** stems and slice mush-rooms in half; set them aside.

2 **CUT** the beef into ½-inch cubes.

3 **COMBINE** the stock and gravy in the saucepan over medium heat. Allow the mixture to come to a boil, then lower the heat and simmer for 15 minutes.

4 **ADD** the peas and carrots and bay leaf, stir, and simmer for an additional 15 minutes; serve over noodles cooked as directed on package.

ONE, TWO, BUCKLE YOUR SHOE.
THREE, FOUR, YOU'VE MADE YOUR STEW!

> 🌸 **FAMILY MOMENT:**
> Make a game out of it and hide the bay leaf in someone's bowl.
> Whoever gets it begins to talk first about his or her
> day and gets a special, or extra, dessert.

Chicken Bean Casserole

The most remarkable thing about my mother is that,
for thirty years, she served the family nothing but leftovers.
The original meal has never been found.

—Calvin Trillin

 Ingredients

- 1 pound boneless, skinless chicken breast
- 1 can (32 ounces) red kidney beans
- 1 tablespoon ketchup
- 2 teaspoons mustard
- 1 can (20 ounces) chopped pineapple

 Tools

Knife

Cutting board

Large rectangular casserole or baking pan

Can opener

Measuring spoons

Mixing spoon

Mixing bowl

☀ TIP:
Serve over rice or noodles.

DIRECTIONS

SERVES
4

1 **PREHEAT** the oven to 350 degrees.

2 **CUT** the chicken breast into cubes.

3 **COMBINE** the chicken, beans, ketchup, mustard, and pineapple in the mixing bowl.

4 **PUT** the mixture into a large casserole or baking pan and bake until chicken is cooked thoroughly, approximately 40 to 45 minutes.

A Surprising Trophy

"**M**om, what are we cooking today?" asked my eight-year-old Alex; he loved to cook. "Something unusual. I noticed a contest in the food section of the newspaper and thought the three of us could conjure up a recipe." I winked at him. "Okay, I'll find Christine." As soon as he dashed from the kitchen, I heard the doorbell ring. "Mom, Bobby's here. Can he cook, too?" asked Alex. "Of course," I answered.

Bobby's Mom and Dad had died in an automobile accident six months earlier. He'd moved in with his grandparents. When I'd prepare a big batch of spaghetti, I'd send half of it over to them.

I removed a can of Hungry Jack biscuits from my refrigerator and tapped it on the counter. Soon, Alex returned with his sister and Bobby. "A can of biscuits," said Christine. "What can we make with biscuits?" "Hungry Jack has a contest for new recipes using its biscuits," I replied.

"So, everyone, put on your thinking caps. The example shows peanut butter and jelly coated with raisins," I instructed. "Yuck," said Christine. "That sounds good," said Alex, who loves peanut butter and jelly. Bobby nodded in agreement. "Let's think healthy, nutritious, and original," I said, knowing that the winning recipe would have to be a blend of unique fillings.

Alex separated the rolls, and Bobby placed them on the baking sheet. "Mom, how about sticking tuna and mustard on them?" asked Alex. "I say we top them with cream cheese and olives," said Christine. She glared at Alex. I opened the oven door and shoved in the tray. "After these bake, you can each try your own ideas." Satisfied, they rifled through the refrigerator for their ingredients. "So what do you win?" asked Christine. "The grand prize is a trip to Florida." "But we already live in Florida," said Alex. "I'd want to go somewhere else." *He's right,* I thought. "Lots of people will enter the contest," I smiled.

"Beep, beep." The oven timer signaled. Christine grabbed a pot holder and removed the tray. "Let them cool and then we will start filling." "Mom, what are you using?" asked Alex. "I am thinking of something vegetarian." Several combinations danced through my mind, such as cheese and broccoli or yogurt and blueberries. Several minutes later, we each layered a couple of flaky biscuits. Without saying a word, Bobby filled his with hot dogs and pickles.

We sampled each other's creations. In the meantime, Christine stuck in a fresh tray to bake. A couple of hours later, the kitchen started to resemble a busy restaurant. Empty cans of biscuits were scattered on the countertops and table. I tried to clear off a spot to record my findings.

The ingredients had to be squeezed into thirteen blank spaces. It was not an easy feat. The children gave me new suggestions. "Let's make little pizzas," said Alex. "Why don't you make minilasagna," said Bobby. "Wonderful idea, Bobby. Alex, you get out the ricotta. Bobby please grate the mozzarella. And Christine, dig up a jar of tomato sauce. I'll bake another tray." After they cooled, Alex spooned on ricotta cheese and Christine topped it with sauce. Bobby sprinkled the mozzarella cheese on the open-face biscuits. We placed them in the oven for five minutes. Soon, the cheese melted and the biscuits crisped. The rich aroma seeped through the kitchen and then drifted through the house. We all sampled the minilasagna.

I revised my format, but I still needed one more ingredient. "How about spinach, Mom?" asked Alex. "I love spinach. My Mom made it with a cream sauce," said Bobby. I saw his eyes glisten. This was the first time he had ever mentioned his mother. "Perfect. Spinach will make this a healthy-type recipe. Let's try it on the remaining biscuits." We layered and baked. Everyone tasted the results and agreed the spinach enhanced the flavor. Then I was able to complete the form.

"Thanks, kids. Tomorrow we'll finish the last section." "Can I come over and help?" asked Bobby. "Certainly! We couldn't have done this without you." I smiled at him, and he giggled.

The next afternoon, we composed the last segment of the contest: explaining why this recipe was our personal favorite. Everyone was excited as I typed up our entry. Before mailing it, the kids and I kissed the envelope for good luck.

Days and weeks passed, and almost three months slipped by with no word. "Mom, Bobby and I were wondering if you heard anything about the contest?" asked Alex. Bobby stared at me, waiting for my answer. "No. I guess someone else won." Both their faces showed disappointment. "We did have fun, didn't we?" "Yes, lots of fun and biscuits," he smiled. "I just wish we'd won." "Me, too," said Bobby. He came over every after-noon now as he felt comfortable in our house.

That same day, the doorbell rang, and I opened it to find a large package. I hadn't ordered anything, but the box was addressed to me. I opened the flaps and glanced inside. An orange basketball stared back at me. I grinned. Curious, I withdrew the ball, and as I rotated it I saw colorful silhouettes of people pitching basketballs and the logo of Hungry Jack in the center. Peering back into the box, I saw a sheet of paper lining the bottom.

It read: "CONGRATULATIONS! Your entry has been selected as one of the 50 First Prizes in the Hungry Jack Biscuits Contest."

We had won! "Alex, Bobby, Christine, everyone come here," I called. They all raced into the kitchen. Alex spotted the ball first. "I guess we won after all." I watched their eyes sparkle as I read the letter. "This is great. I prayed we'd win. I can't wait to tell my Grandma," said Bobby. His face glittered like a Christmas tree. "I couldn't have done it without you three."

"Can we play with it?" asked Alex, grinning at Bobby. "Of course, you can!" They dashed outdoors to slam-dunk that new basketball.

Receiving the surprise trophy validated our afternoon bonding experience, especially for Bobby. His soul took a giant step toward healing and accepting the death of his parents, and I was grateful to play a part in mending the void in a little boy's heart.

—*Suzanne Baginskie*

Lasagna Biscuits

Lasagna: The world's most perfect food.

—Garfield

🛒 INGREDIENTS

- 1 can (16 ounces) of biscuits
- 1 tablespoon olive oil
- 1 package (6 ounces) fresh spinach
- ½ cup ricotta cheese
- 1 large jar (1 pound 12 ounces) marinara sauce
- 1 cup shredded or grated mozzarella cheese

TOOLS

Measuring cup

Saucepan

Steamer insert

Spreading spatula

Baking sheet pan

DIRECTIONS

⏱ SPEEDY TIP:
This is a quick substitute for the real deal.

1 PREHEAT the oven to 400 degrees.

2 SEPARATE and bake the biscuits according to the package directions; when cooled, separate each biscuit into halves.

3 STEAM the spinach, cool slightly, and squeeze out any excess water. Set it aside.

4 SPOON some ricotta cheese onto each biscuit and spread it evenly, then add a layer of spinach. Spoon on the marinara sauce, then top with a sprinkle of mozzarella cheese.

5 PLACE the biscuits on the baking sheet pan and bake for 5 to 8 minutes, or until the cheese melts.

Barley Soup

Worries go down better with soup.

—A Jewish proverb

🛒 Ingredients

- 2 carrots
- 1 small onion, peeled
- 2 pieces celery
- 1 potato, peeled
- ¾ cup pearl barley, uncooked
- 1 teaspoon dried basil
- ½ teaspoon dried oregano
- 7 cups water
- 1 can (14 ounces) crushed tomatoes
- 1 tablespoon salt
- ½ teaspoon black pepper

Tools

Knife

Cutting board

Small mixing bowl

Mixing spoon

Saucepan

Measuring spoons

Measuring cups

Can opener

> **🧑‍🍳 VARIATION:**
> Add some cooked, cut-up beef and sliced mushrooms.

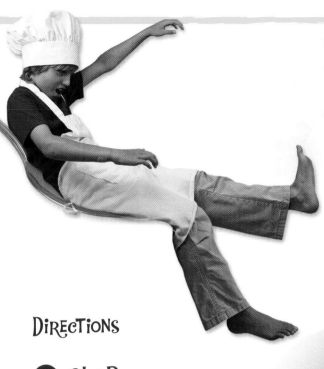

DIRECTIONS

1 **CHOP** the carrots, onion, celery, and potato into smallpieces; keep them in the small mixing bowl.

2 **IN** the saucepan, combine the barley, basil, oregano, water, tomatoes, salt, and pepper. Add the vegetables and stir.

3 **LET** the mixture come to a boil on high heat, then simmer it on low heat for approximately 1½ hours, or until the barley is very tender.

NOODLE PUDDING

🛒 INGREDIENTS

- 12 ounces of noodles, uncooked
- Butter or vegetable oil for greasing the pan
- 1¼ cups sour cream

- 1½ cups cottage cheese
- 3 eggs
- ¼ teaspoon nutmeg
- ¼ teaspoon salt
- 2 tablespoons melted butter

🏺 TOOLS

Pasta pot

Mixing bowl

Mixing spoon

Measuring cups

Measuring spoons

Large rectangular baking pan

SERVES 6-8

> 💡 **TIP:**
> Serve this at room temperature as a side dish with almost anything else.

DIRECTIONS

1 **COOK** the noodles as directed on the package. Drain.

2 **PREHEAT** the oven to 350 degrees.

3 **GREASE** the baking pan. Add cooked noodles.

4 **MIX** the sour cream, cottage cheese, eggs, nutmeg, salt, and melted butter in the mixing bowl and then pour the mixture over the noodles in the prepared pan.

5 **BAKE** for approximately 45 minutes.

BBQ Ribs

Get out your brush and get artistic here with barbeque sauce, like my nephew does, and get creative.

🛒 INGREDIENTS

- 4 racks baby back ribs
- 1 gallon water
- 4 cups barbecue sauce

🥄 TOOLS

Measuring cups

Large saucepan

Baking sheet pan

Dining is, and always was a great artistic opportunity.

—Frank Lloyd Wright

DIRECTIONS

1 PLACE the ribs in the large saucepan.

> ☼ **TIP:**
> Use Handi-Wipes instead of napkins to clean the messy hands and faces you'll get from this delicious dish.

2 POUR the water and 1 cup of the barbecue sauce over the ribs and make sure they are all covered; if not, add more water.

3 BRING the ribs and sauce to a boil, and then simmer them for 1 hour. Remove the ribs from the saucepan and drain off any excess liquid.

SERVES
4

4 PLACE the ribs face down on the baking sheet pan and brush on half of the remaining barbecue sauce.

5 ROAST for 30 minutes at 350 degrees. Remove the pan from the oven and flip over the ribs. Coat the other side with the remaining barbecue sauce and return the ribs to the oven for another 30 minutes.

6 TURN off the oven and keep the ribs in it for another 20 minutes. Then take them out and enjoy 'em!

NONA'S GARDEN

When my grandparents emigrated from Italy to the United States, they joined the rest of their clan who'd already settled in the small town of Oelwein, Iowa, where the men had found jobs working for the railroad. Because the majority of Oelwein's population was of German descent, my family had a hard time fitting in. So, to give them a sense of the familiar, of community and belonging, until they "learned the ropes," the heads of each family pooled their money and bought a square city block of homes.

Italians love their gardens, so when my relatives settled into their new homes, the backyard fences came down and all that open space became flower and vegetable gardens. Cobbled pathways connected each house, and grape arbors, bearing the fruit from which fine wine is made, shaded them.

"What's wrong?" Nona, my grandmother, asked me one day when she'd caught me sulking in my room.

"Nothing," I said, not wanting to tell. The truth was too painful. I was tired of being the brunt of jokes at the playground. Tired of being the "different" girl everybody picked on because of my dark coloring and simple, handmade clothes.

"You got nothing to do?" she said. "Then you come with me." There was no saying "no" to Nona. I knew she knew what was wrong, and it was lesson time. I set my stubborn jaw and followed her downstairs, where she snatched up her basket and garden shears. "You come," she said again.

We headed toward the herb garden first, a sunny spot that shot up against Zia Amalia's zucchini patch.

"See here?" Nona said, pointing to a thick bush, its rangy stems lifted toward the sun. "This is oregano."

Snip went the shears, and a handful of stems and leaves went into the basket. "Look," she said. "See the leaves? Small. Hardly anything to them."

She waited for me to nod in agreement. "Smell." She rubbed a few teardrop-shaped oregano leaves between her fingers and wafted them beneath my nose. "Remember the smell," she said.

"Huh?" I blurted, wondering what she meant. It wasn't like I didn't already know what these plants were. I'd helped her put the seedlings in the ground last spring.

She moved to the next row of bushes, looking much like an ambitious bee in search of nectar. "This is rosemary," she informed me, stooping to clip a lush frond stiff with spiky leaves. Again she crushed a couple of leaves between her fingers and made me inhale the scent. "Remember," she said.

Next came the basil plants, light green and dew-kissed glossy, their familiar scent the sweetest of all. We repeated the procedure. I was wondering if Nona would ever just get to the point and let me go back to my sulking.

"Very different from the other two, eh?" she pointed out, snipping and tossing a few more bunches of basil into her basket. This time she didn't wait for me to answer. Instead, with me still in reluctant tow, she left the herb plot to gather several ripe tomatoes, a fat-to-near-bursting head of garlic, and three purple eggplants.

"We make *melanzani parmiggiano* for supper tonight," she announced. "Your favorite."

Back inside the house, she tossed me an apron and asked me to rinse off the vegetables. I groaned.

"You got nothing else to do," she said. "You help me make the supper."

When the cleaned herbs and produce sat drying on dish towels, Nona said, "We start with the tomatoes. We peel the skins and put them in a pot to simmer." "Look," she said. "They're very different from the eggplants, no?"

No kidding, I thought. *Any dummy can see that.*

She peeled and sliced the eggplant into fat rounds, dipped them first in beaten egg and then in seasoned bread crumbs, then fried them till golden in olive oil flavored with the fresh minced garlic we'd picked. After laying them flat in a baking dish, she turned her attention back to the simmering tomatoes.

"Now we add the herbs," she said, showing me what to do and how to do it. We stripped the leaves from the stems of each different herb and divided them into three separate piles.

"Take a palm full of basil leaves," she said and then watched me carefully as I obeyed. "Rub them between your hands and toss them in the pot. *Bene.* Don't it make your hands smell good? Now the oregano. Rub those, too. See the tiny leaves and the different smells." Helplessly, I looked at her and shrugged my shoulders. "And now the rosemary," she winked. "Just a little kiss from Signorina Rosemary. Smell how strong her breath is?" Nona smiled at my groan. "Good. This dish is going to be perfect. Toss."

I helped her slice the cheeses, and then we assembled the casserole in layers of eggplant, cheese, and tomato sauce.

And somewhere along the line, much to my amazement, I realized I was enjoying myself.

That evening after the blessing, Nona served the dish we'd made. The casserole's aroma settled around the table like perfume from heaven. My family dug in.

"Well," Nona said, her bright brown eyes snagging mine as I chewed my first hefty mouthful. "What did you learn today, granddaughter?"

"I don't know, Nona. What did I learn?" I teased. Of course I'd learned a lesson today, and she knew me well enough to know I'd gotten her point long before we'd finished preparing our supper.

"Okay, smart girl, I tell you. Every living thing is different in my garden," she said. I giggled. To Nona, plants had personalities, lives uniquely theirs, just like people.

"Nobody the same as nobody else, see? But when you and me put everybody together today, we got something special. Something delicious."

"Yeah, we did," I admitted, a rush of emotion pooling in my eyes. And that was the shining moment in which the "different" person I was committed herself to taking joy in every one of the unique differences that made me.

"God is very wise," Nona said. "Remember that always."

—Paula L. Silici

Mashed Potato Casserole

Ingredients

- 10 medium potatoes, sliced
- 1 cup sour cream
- 1 tablespoon grated onion
- ½ cup (1 stick) butter
- 1 teaspoon salt
- ¼ cup grated Parmesan cheese
- ¼ teaspoon pepper
- Butter or vegetable oil for greasing the pan

SERVES 4

Tools

Large casserole dish

Measuring cups

Measuring spoon

Mixing spoon

Masher or electric hand mixer

Mixing bowl

Peeler

Saucepan

Colander

> ☀ **TIP:**
> Add some cooked ground beef to the bottom of the casserole to make a quick and easy version of English shepherd's pie.

DIRECTIONS

1 **PEEL** the potatoes and boil them in water until tender.

2 **DRAIN** the potatoes, place them in the mixing bowl, and mash them until almost smooth (I like some little lumps).

3 **PREHEAT** the oven to 350 degrees.

4 **ADD** the sour cream, onion, butter, salt, Parmesan cheese, and pepper and mix with the spoon.

5 **GREASE** a casserole dish and spoon the mixture into it.

6 **SPRINKLE** the potato mixture with a little extra Parmesan cheese.

7 **BAKE** for 30 minutes.

#4 **MASHED POTATOES**—These should be made by several pairs of hands. They beg for that. So if Grandma cooks the potatoes right, and they're warm but not too hot to handle, that's where you come in. That's when you can peel away the potato skins, let the insides tumble out into a bowl, and add two of the best things in the world: butter and milk. That's when we take forks and mash and mash and mash until we get that special smooth, glistening mashed potato fluff that goes into a bowl and onto the table. And right into your tummies. . . .

Why wouldn't the reporter leave the mashed potatoes alone?

He desperately wanted a scoop!

The Royal Baker and Pasties

My granddaughter, Aimee, swimming in my apron, bent over the kitchen counter. She and I were creating a modern-day version of the northern Michigan miner's supper-sandwich called the "pasty." My granddaughter wanted to make her pasties even better than mine.

She thought my method was not creative enough. So, after carefully seasoning her creation with salt and pepper and topping it with margarine, she sealed her pastry with a flair—pressing a fork around the edges, rather than just pressing the edges together like I had. When I began copying Aimee with my fork, her giggles rose and she upped the competition a notch.

Aimee took a chunk of her dough and used the edge of a spoon to cut the simple shapes of a flower and a leaf, wet them, and pressed them artistically on another pasty. Her brother and cousins, when they made pasties, simply pressed the dough together, but this was Aimee, proving her uniqueness.

Whenever I made pasties with my grandchildren, I shared stories of the recipe's background, as well as mine, so that with each recipe came adventure, questions, and lots of giggles. I told tales of miners' wives baking a treat, like apple preserves, in one end of a pasty for an all-in-one meal. I described the mine near the town where I had grown up, and we discussed rocks, ores, and their uses.

We cooked as we talked, and we were done cooking before we knew it. We unveiled the finished pasties. For our friendly competition, Grandpa judged (and threatened to eat) each pasty. We both sighed an appreciative "Ohhh" when viewing Aimee's creative masterpieces, which I truthfully and cheerfully admitted had turned out better than mine.

"I win. I win!" Aimee shouted, as Grandpa dubbed her the "Royal Baker" by tapping each flour-covered shoulder with a clean spatula.

Later, after thinking about the evening, I thought, *No, I win.* I felt like I had been awarded the "grand prize"—a hug from the Royal Baker and another lifetime memory!

—*Delores Liesner*

Pasties

Underground miners used to carry pasties close to their bodies to stay warm. Pasties are a wonderful food that can stay warm for hours—and can warm your heart and soul.

🛒 Ingredients

- 4 large potatoes
- 4 carrots
- 1 onion
- 8 refrigerated piecrusts
- 1 pound cooked ground beef
- 4 teaspoons margarine
- ½ teaspoon salt
- ¼ teaspoon pepper
- Nonstick cooking spray

🍶 Tools

Food processor

Measuring spoons

Cutting board

Baking sheet pan

Mixing bowl

Peeler

Knife

Fork

Serves 6–8

DIRECTIONS

1 **PEEL** and quarter the potatoes, carrots, and onion; chop them in the food processor and transfer them to the mixing bowl.

2 **PREHEAT** the oven to 350 degrees.

3 **CUT** each piecrust in half and lay the halves on a counter or table.

4 **PLACE** ½ cup of the vegetables slightly off center on each crust; put about 2 ounces of ground beef on top of each portion of vegetables, and then top each portion with ½ teaspoon margarine. Sprinkle with salt and pepper; fold and seal the pasty by pressing the edges together with a fork.

5 **SPRAY** the baking sheet pan with the nonstick cooking spray, then place the pasties on the pan.

6 **MAKE** two ½-inch slits on top of each pasty.

7 **BAKE** for 25 minutes, or until golden brown.

QUESADILLAS

SERVES 3-4

🛒 INGREDIENTS

- 2 cups chicken, cooked
- 4 teaspoons vegetable oil
- 8 6-inch flour tortillas
- 1 cup grated Cheddar cheese
- 1 cup grated Monterey Jack cheese

🥄 TOOLS

Knife

Cutting board (or other cutting surface)

Measuring spoons

Measuring cups

Frying pan

🌹 FAMILY MOMENT:

Make it a Mexican night. Dress in a poncho and sombrero. Dance to Mexican music and play your maracas.

Directions

1 **CUT** the chicken into cubes.

2 **IN** the frying pan on low heat, heat 1 teaspoon of oil. Add a tortilla, then some chicken, then ¼ cup of the Cheddar cheese and ¼ cup of the Monterey Jack cheese. Then place another flour tortilla on top of the cheeses.

3 **CONTINUE** cooking on low heat until golden brown on one side, then flip the quesadilla with a pancake turner and brown the other side.

4 **REMOVE** the quesadilla to a cutting board and let it sit for 5 minutes.

5 **REPEAT** with the remaining tortillas.

6 **CUT** each quesadilla into quarters and enjoy.

☀ SERVING TIP:
Serve these with sour cream, guacamole, and some lime wedges.

LOVE SOUP EMERGENCY

"This calls for a double recipe of Love Soup," I say aloud to myself while hanging up the telephone. Someone special needed dinner. I could make a double batch of Love Soup. My own family could enjoy a good lunch, and we'd have enough to share. Double the recipe, double the love.

"Who was on the phone, Mom?" my little daughter asks.

"Someone special needs a meal. Can you help me make a double batch of Love Soup?" My little girl hurries to the recipe box, flips through the cards, and, like a magician pulling a rabbit out of a hat, waves a tattered card with the notation "Grandma's Love Soup." Barely legible, the careful handwriting on the card is smeared with years of use. A splotch of tomato juice here, grime from ground beef grease there. The edges of the card are frayed, even charred where I once carelessly left it too near the back burner.

"Double the recipe," I read aloud from the card, "double the love. Three pounds of ground beef, six cans of stewed tomatoes, chicken broth. . . . Do I have enough broth? Honey, will you chop the carrots? The younger kids can chop celery. The older kids will brown the hamburger." We get to work—all seven of us—making a double batch of Grandma's Love Soup.

For over twenty years my mother has been preparing Love Soup. The recipe is simple, substantial, freezes well, and has great potential for "doubling": one for our family and one for someone else who may need a meal.

If a friend was ill, Love Soup in a recycled ice cream bucket was just the cure. If an elderly neighbor was experiencing loneliness, Love Soup and a chat were just the thing. If a friend gave birth to a baby, Love Soup would nourish her new family.

As I grew up, I counted on Love Soup for comfort. When I broke up with a boyfriend, Love Soup helped heal the wound. When I married and delivered my babies, Love Soup filled up my family so I could rest. My mother's soup became legendary. Over the years, I made many attempts to replicate her recipe.

Now my kids and I cook together on a mission to create a meal for someone in need. We spend a good part of the morning simmering, cooling, and skimming. "Job's done, Mom! The bucket is ready for recycling!" they holler. I ladle the soup into the clean ice cream bucket, seal the top, and stash the meal in a grocery bag. I toss in a loaf of homemade bread and a bagged salad, just the way my mother would have. "Now we've got dinner prepared for later, and we still have time to respond to the Love Soup Emergency," I tell my kids. "Double the recipe, double the love."

Balancing the grocery bag on the passenger-side seat, the kids and I load into our vehicle. "Who's the Love Soup for, Mommy?" asks my curious preschooler.

"It's a surprise! Someone really needs lunch," I assure my girl.

"I'll bet they never tasted soup as good as ours, Mom," boasts my kindergartener.

"I don't know about that," I smile into the rearview mirror at my gang.

Thirty miles later, I turn our vehicle onto a familiar street, careful not to topple the loaded grocery bag. In an instant, my children begin bouncing up and down in their seats like bubbles in boiling water.

"Grandma's!" they all squeal in a chorus of delight. "Yes, someone needed Grandma's Love Soup today and that someone is Grandma!" they yell and tumble out of the truck.

My mom embraces each of my children and graciously accepts my second-rate version of her exquisite soup. We spend some time catching up, playing, and enjoying the day. But before we leave for home, my mother calls out from her front steps, "It's almost dinnertime! The kids will be hungry when you get home."

I roll down my driver's-side window and call out, "Don't worry Mom, I doubled the recipe! There's plenty at home for us."

Waving and smiling, my mother nods, "Of course you did." Double the recipe, double the love.

—*Cristy Trandahl*

VEGETABLE-HAMBURGER SOUP

My mom made this soup for me when I was growing up and came inside from the cold and snow.

🛒 INGREDIENTS

- 1 tablespoon oil
- 1 onion, chopped
- 1 pound ground beef
- Garlic powder—to taste
- 2 large cans chicken broth
- 2 cans (14 ounces each) mixed vegetables
- 3 potatoes, cut into cubes
- 2 carrots, cut into little pieces
- Salt and pepper

🧂 TOOLS

Cutting board

Measuring spoons

Mixing spoon

Can opener

Saucepan

Knife

SERVES 4–6

DIRECTIONS

1 **IN** the saucepan, heat the oil over medium heat and brown the onion slightly.

2 **ADD** the ground beef and brown it.

3 **ADD** the garlic powder, chicken broth, mixed vegetables, potatoes, carrots, and salt and pepper to taste.

4 **COOK** for about 45 minutes. If more liquid is needed, add hot water.

💡 **TIP:**
You can use canned or frozen mixed vegetables in this recipe.

SEEING EYES MOM

"Kyle, put that cookie back! Dinner is only ten minutes away," I commanded over my shoulder as I snapped spaghetti into the bubbling pot.

With a guilty jerk, my six-year-old clanked down the lid to the cookie canister. "How did you know what I was doing, Mommy?"

Dropping a kiss on my cheek as he passed through the kitchen, my husband grinned. "Because moms have eyes in the back of their heads." He winked at me and added, "That's how they keep track of their kids."

Aided by shadows, reflections in mirrors and microwave, and by corner-of-the-eye glimpses, I was able to catch my four young children in a variety of acts. It wasn't long before they became true believers: Mom could "see all."

Several days later, I was again frantic during that after-school, before-dinner-hour rush. Cramped for time by an evening church meeting, I popped frozen lasagna into the oven and began washing salad greens.

Three-year-old Kayla tugged on my arm and thrust a paper at me. "Look, Mommy. See my picture?"

"Umm, that's nice," I agreed absently. Without even bothering to look down, I reached for the loaf of garlic bread.

"But Mommy—"

"Yes, Kayla, good job," I murmured from the depths of the knife drawer. I grabbed the slender, serrated knife.

"No, Mommy," she demanded. "Not with your back eyes. Look with your front eyes!"

A bit amused—if irritated—by her insistence, I heaved a massive sigh. I turned and reached for the drawing. "How pretty," I gushed to mask my indifference. "A colorful rainbow!"

"I used every crayon in the box," she boasted. And she had. Even black and brown.

"And you put a heart at the end of it." I stopped. "A pink heart. A heart with eyes—and a smile."

Kayla's proud grin stretched as wide as the bread platter. She nodded her agreement and skipped away.

The heart stared up at me from the page. I felt accused. Guilty. Convicted.

Was I in such a hurry that by not seeing I also didn't feel? Was I missing today in pursuit of tomorrow?

How often, I wondered, *had I neglected my "front eyes?" How often had I slighted my little ones—quashed their endless queries, neglected their penetrating thoughts, disregarded their insightful comments? How many times had eager little hands literally grabbed my face to point me in the right direction?*

Soon enough, my children would discover that I have no extra eyes in the back of my head. Meanwhile, I vowed to focus. I wanted my family to live in a house where eyes see and ears hear.

By using my "front eyes," I knew I would see with my smiling heart.

—*Carol McAdoo Rehme*

SPAGHETTI PIE

#5 **SPAGHETTI**—Is there anything as wonderfully weird as spaghetti? It starts out as yellow sticks so skinny you can barely hold them. Then you plop those sticks in boiling water, and in a few minutes you have something soft and smooth and yummy. That yummy stuff then gets mixed up with little round meatballs and goes swimming in bright red tomato sauce that gets all over your face and gives you a spicy red mustache.

🛒 INGREDIENTS

- 6 ounces uncooked spaghetti
- 2 tablespoons margarine
- ⅓ cup grated Parmesan cheese
- 2 eggs, well beaten
- 1 cup cottage cheese
- Butter *or* vegetable oil for greasing the pie plate
- 1 pound ground beef
- 1 can (8 ounces) tomato sauce
- ½ teaspoon dried basil
- ¼ teaspoon garlic powder
- ½ cup grated mozzarella cheese

🫗 TOOLS

Pasta pot

Colander

Mixing bowl

Measuring cups

Measuring
  spoons

Mixing spoon

10-inch pie plate

Frying pan

> ☀️ **TIP:**
> Put a little tomato sauce on the side for a little dipping fun!

DiRections

1 PREhEaT the oven to 350 degrees.

SERVES
4-6

2 COOK the spaghetti according to the package directions and drain.

3 PLaCE the cooked spaghetti in the mixing bowl with the margarine, Parmesan cheese, and eggs. Grease the 10-inch pie plate and spoon the spaghetti mixture into it to form the piecrust.

4 SPREaD the cottage cheese on the pasta layer.

5 IN the frying pan over medium heat, cook the ground beef until browned. Then add the tomato sauce, basil, and garlic powder; pour this mixture over the cheese layer.

6 BakE uncovered for 20 minutes.

7 SPRiNKLE with the grated mozzarella cheese. Return the pie to the oven for 5 minutes, or until cheese melts.

ChiNESE PizZa

I pulled the tiny red suitcase off my twin bed and stormed toward the front door. I reached up to grab the doorknob and make my escape, and I waited for someone to notice I was leaving—for good.

My mother casually asked where I was going at night, all by myself. I told her of all of the injustices I had suffered as the youngest child in the family. I tearfully announced my decision to strike out on my own. At the ripe old age of six, I was officially running away from home.

My mother listened patiently and asked if I were headed for any place in particular. I didn't hesitate. "Red China."

To her credit, she didn't even blink.

I had some vague idea that if I walked to the end of my city street and made a left at the steep hill where my sisters and I always went sleigh riding, I would eventually end up in the mysterious Far East.

"That's quite a long journey," she commented gently.

I was willing to linger a few more minutes and tell her more about my plans. After all, I wouldn't be seeing my family for a long time once I reached Red China.

"I know," I whispered.

"Do you have enough clothes packed?"

"Yes." I had one extra polo shirt and my favorite pink and white nightgown. I also had my dolly. I was ready to go.

"Is Betsy Wetsy going with you?"

"Yes."

"Well, I'm glad she's going with you to keep you company on such a long journey. Red China is very far away, and you'll be traveling for quite a while. Are you sure you want to start on your journey in the dark?"

I hesitated as I pondered my lonely adventure. "I think so."

My mother thought for a moment. "Since you have such a big trip ahead of you, would you and Betsy Wetsy like to stay and have dinner with the family before you leave?"

"Well, maybe." I thought it over. "What's for dinner?"

"Pizza."

Even at the tender age of six, I knew you couldn't get good New York pizza in Red China. Tossing my suitcase aside, Betsy and I gladly stayed for dinner that night, and the next, and the next, never to arrive at Red China.

—*Pamela Hackett Hobson*

Oriental Beef

Ingredients

- 1 tablespoon olive oil
- 1½ pounds ground beef
- 1 package onion soup mix
- 1½ cups boiling water
- ⅔ cup sliced celery
- 1 can bean sprouts, drained
- 1½ tablespoons soy sauce
- 1 can (10¾ ounces) cream of mushroom soup
- 2 tablespoons sesame seeds
- 1 cup uncooked rice

Tools

Large casserole dish

Measuring cups

Measuring spoons

Mixing spoon

Frying pan

Saucepan

DIRECTIONS

1 **PREHEAT** the oven to 350 degrees.

2 **IN** the frying pan, brown the ground beef in the olive oil on medium heat.

3 **COMBINE** the onion soup mix and water in the saucepan and heat it to boiling, then add the celery, rice, bean sprouts, soy sauce, soup, and sesame seeds. Add beef. Mix thoroughly.

4 **POUR** the mixture into the large casserole dish. Bake for about 70 minutes, or until the rice is tender.

Snow Memories

The day after the blizzard, my dad shoveled our sidewalk and piled mountains of snow parallel to the street. My parents dressed my sister and me in snow pants, coats, and boots. We went out to play and jumped from one mound of snow to the next.

My mom and dad, sitting by the window, watched us with such joy in their eyes. After a while, Dad came outside, puffed up in his snow clothes, and gave us new, dry gloves. Despite the cold, my sister and I loved to play, and even after my Dad went back into the house, we made snow angels and snowmen for hours and hours.

After a long time, Dad called us in, and we changed our clothes. We sat in front of our small coal stove, which we called "Big Bertha," and waited patiently for Dad to finish preparing his delicious, homemade soup. We were cold, our hands were bright red and chapped, and we knew that the savory soup would warm us.

While Dad finished the soup, Mom arranged orange peels on the stove, and they lent a wonderful, sweet smell to the room. We also used Big Bertha to roast the most delicious chestnuts. Everything smelled *so good!*

My mom tuned the radio to *Amos 'N' Andy,* and as we listened the snow started up again. My family gathered around the table, and, while my sister and I stared out the kitchen window, watching the snow whirling in our yard, my dad poured the fragrant soup into our bowls. At last, we got our soup, and even though it was so cold outside, we felt very warm sharing dinner with our family!

Remembering nights like this still makes me feel warm and fuzzy. And every time my children, and now my grandchildren, make this soup, I remember my dad standing over Big Bertha, adding his finishing touches to our soup. Every family needs its finishing touches.

—*Valeri Frontera*

"It is curious that dad puts on about 30 pounds at this time every year."

Reprinted by permission of Jonny Hawkins. ©2007 Jonny Hawkins.

Mexican Pita Pizza

 **Ingredients**

- 4 6-inch pitas
- 1⅓ cups salsa
- 2 cups shredded Monterey Jack cheese

Tools

Baking sheet pan

Measuring cups

Mixing spoon

> 💡 **TIP:**
> Make these ahead of time and refrigerate them. When you're nearly ready to eat, heat them in the microwave.

Have a Fiesta!

SERVES 4

DIRECTIONS

1 **PREHEAT** the oven to 350 degrees.

2 **PLACE** the pitas on the baking sheet pan.

3 **DIVIDE** the salsa among the four pitas.

4 **PLACE** ½ cup shredded cheese on each pita pizza.

5 **BAKE** for 10 to 15 minutes, or until the cheese is all melted.

CHEEZ-IT® CHICKEN

 INGREDIENTS

- 1 box (10 ounces) Cheez-It® crackers
- 8 ounces butter
- 4 to 6 boneless, skinless chicken breasts
- Butter or vegetable oil for greasing the pan

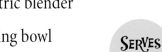 TOOLS

Electric blender

Mixing bowl

Saucepan

Large rectangular baking pan

SERVES
4

DiReCTioNS

1 **PRehEaT** the oven to 350 degrees.

💡 **TIP:**
Any cracker will do in this recipe as long as it is tasty.

2 **ChOP** the Cheez-It® crackers in the blender to make crumbs; set them aside in the mixing bowl. If needed, crush more.

3 **MELT** the butter over low heat; dip each chicken breast into the melted butter, then into the Cheez-It® crumbs.

4 **GREaSE** the baking pan.

5 **PLaCE** the chicken breasts in the pan. Bake for 1 hour.

"But I Don't Like Tomatoes!"

Cooking is such a passion of mine. I love to share it with my grandson whenever I have the opportunity. But one day, five-year-old Aaron, who had already declared his nutritional likes and dislikes to me on many occasions, expressed a definite lack of enthusiasm for our cooking project.

"You've eaten Grandma's soup before, haven't you?"

Aaron sighed and searched his mind, his big brown eyes registering the memory. "Yes, but I don't remember seeing any tomatoes."

Little ones can be so adamant, and eating a variety of healthy foods is not high on their what-can-I-do-for-fun-today list.

"Why don't we read the recipe, and see what it says?" I responded calmly, as I pulled down the cookbook I planned to use and set up the step stool for him. I thumbed through the food-splattered pages, while Aaron dragged the stool a little closer to the counter and climbed up on it.

"What does your recipe say, Grandma?" I placed an apron over his head, brushed his tousled hair back from his eyes, and gently kissed his forehead. I glanced down at the page and began reciting the ingredients almost by rote while continuing to secure the apron ties around his tummy with a bow.

"Two tablespoons of butter, but we're going to use olive oil instead because it's healthier for us." Aaron studied my face seriously and nodded his approval—my blue linen apron almost touching his toes.

"Let me see—what else? An onion, a clove of garlic, and—oh look, I have some broccoli and baby potatoes—I think we'll throw them in as well." Aaron stared at the open page as though he were reading the recipe along with me, glancing up at my face occasionally.

I moved to and fro between the refrigerator and pantry, gathering our ingredients while he stood, waiting patiently on the step stool, inspecting each vegetable as I placed it on the kitchen counter. He was my only grand-child—my heart. And I wanted him to experience all that was good and kind in the world. Baking cookies might be fun and satisfy his sweet tooth, but I hoped to ignite the cooking gene in him and to help instill the importance of eating healthfully at the same time.

"We'll have to chop up everything," I said, adding carrots and celery to the growing pile of vegetables on the counter. As I reached into an overhead cupboard for some seasonings, I noticed that Aaron's attention had turned toward the chicken broth and can of Italian tomatoes that I had just set down.

"Grandma, do we have to put in tomatoes?"

I pulled down the oregano and my salt and pepper mills. "Now where's the basil hiding?" I tried to keep the moment light and continued to search my spice rack.

"Well, I think we should, because the recipe tells us to." Aaron wrinkled his little button nose, and his face struck a pout. "So, we'll make it the way the recipe says, and if you don't like it, Grandma will find something else for you to eat." His sweet trusting face melted my heart. "What do you think?" He sighed again and nodded his agreement.

I began to think that baking cookies would have been a whole lot easier, but I started preparing the vegetables anyway. As I chopped I made up counting songs, and Aaron sorted the veggies into separate piles while he nibbled on a piece of carrot.

After I had sautéed the onion and garlic for several minutes I said, "Okay, sweetheart, you can add the carrots now." Vegetable by vegetable I motioned to Aaron, and he added each chopped ingredient to the pot. He was so wrapped up in the moment that when it became time for us to add the tomatoes, he seemed to have completely forgotten his misgivings.

The broth began to boil. I added some seasonings, reduced the heat, and handed Aaron a big wooden spoon. "Now give the soup a stir, my darling, and then we'll put the lid back on and wait for it to cook."

Some thirty minutes later the aroma of freshly cooked vegetables and chicken broth wafted from the kitchen and triggered our taste buds.

"Grandma, I'm getting hungry!"

"It must be time to finish the soup then."

Aaron followed me back into the kitchen. "What do we need to do?" he asked, as I helped him climb back onto the step stool.

While reaching for my blender, I said, "You'll push the button on the blender when I tell you—and then the soup will be finished."

He watched quietly as I carefully ladled the steaming mixture into my blender, made sure the lid was on tight, and showed him which button to push. The appliance whirred and churned into action, first chopping, then puréeing all the vegetables until they became a smooth mélange of individually unrecognizable vegetables.

Aaron's little face beamed proudly as he declared, "This soup smells very good!" Eager to taste the soup he had just helped to prepare—and still wearing my apron—he climbed down from the step stool and asked, "Can we taste it now?"

I filled two bowls for us and sat down beside my grandson who had already made himself comfortable at the kitchen table.

I handed him a spoon and said, "Be careful. It may still be a little too hot, so blow on it before you take a bite, okay?"

He nodded and gently blew on his soup-filled spoon, then gingerly took a small mouthful. After a couple of bites my grandson's face broke into a big grin and his eyes twinkled mischievously.

"You know what Grandma? I think I do like tomatoes!"

—*Gillian White*

Chicken in a Pan

🛒 Ingredients

- ¼ cup olive oil
- 2 pounds boneless, skinless chicken breasts
- ½ teaspoon garlic powder
- ¼ teaspoon salt
- ¼ teaspoon pepper
- 3 pounds red potatoes
- 1 can (29 ounces) crushed tomatoes
- 2 teaspoons basil
- 1 teaspoon oregano

🥄 Tools

Large roasting pan

Measuring spoons

Knife

DiRECTiONS

SERVES
6

① **PREhEaT** the oven to 350 degrees.

② **ADD** the olive oil to the roasting pan; then arrange the chicken breasts on top of the oil. Sprinkle the chicken with the garlic powder, salt, and pepper.

③ **SLiCE** the potatoes and place them on top of the chicken.

④ **POUR** the tomatoes over the potatoes.

⑤ **SPRiNKLE** the basil and oregano on the tomatoes.

⑥ **BaKE** for approximately 2 hours.

> ☼ **TIP:**
> Throw in some frozen
> mixed vegetables to make
> this a meal in one.

STiR-FRiED ChiCKEN

H ave you always wanted to go to Hong Kong?
Well you can—right in your own dining room.
Dress in your favorite kimono and eat with chopsticks.
Don't forget your pet dragon! Hong Kong is closer than you
think—and there's a Disneyland there.

SERVES 4

 INGREDIENTS

- 1 pound skinless, boneless chicken breasts
- 2 tablespoons soy sauce
- 1 teaspoon sesame oil
- 2 tablespoons oil
- 1 tablespoon grated fresh ginger
- 1 can (15 ounces) creamed corn
- 1 cup fresh corn kernels
- 1 teaspoon sesame seeds

 TOOLS

Knife

Cutting board

Bowl or plastic bag

Covered glass dish

Wok or large saucepan

Stirring spoon

Measuring cups

Measuring spoons

Directions

1 CUT the chicken breasts into cubes; place them in a bowl or plastic bag. Add the soy sauce and sesame oil. Marinate overnight in a covered glass dish.

2 IN a wok or large saucepan, add the oil and heat it. Slowly add the chicken. Cook the chicken until brown, stirring occasionally.

3 ADD the ginger, creamed corn, fresh corn, and sesame seeds. Simmer on low heat for 15 minutes.

SERVING SUGGESTION:
Serve over noodles or rice. If you like, substitute beef for the chicken and serve it over brown rice.

Tater Tots® Bake

🛒 INGREDIENTS

- 2 pounds browned ground beef
- 1 can (10¾ ounces) cream of onion soup
- 2 cups grated Cheddar cheese, divided
- 2 pounds frozen Tater Tots®

🥄 TOOLS

Large rectangular baking pan or casserole dish

Measuring cup

Aluminum foil

SERVES 8–10

> ☝ **VARIATION:**
> Instead of the cream of onion soup, use cream of mushroom, cream of celery, or cream of tomato soup.

DIRECTIONS

1 **PREHEAT** the oven to 375 degrees.

2 **BUTTER** a large rectangular baking pan or casserole dish. Place the ground beef on the bottom of the pan.

3 **SPREAD** the soup over the beef.

4 **SPRINKLE** 1 cup of the Cheddar cheese over the mixture.

5 **TOP** with the Tater Tots.

6 **COVER** with aluminum foil and bake for 45 minutes.

7 **UNCOVER** and top with the remaining 1 cup of grated Cheddar cheese. Bake for another 15 minutes until the cheese is golden brown and melted.

Why did the potato cross the road?

He saw a fork up ahead.

Dinner Maze

Chef Antonio is lost and needs to make dinner for his family.
Please help him find his way back into the kitchen.

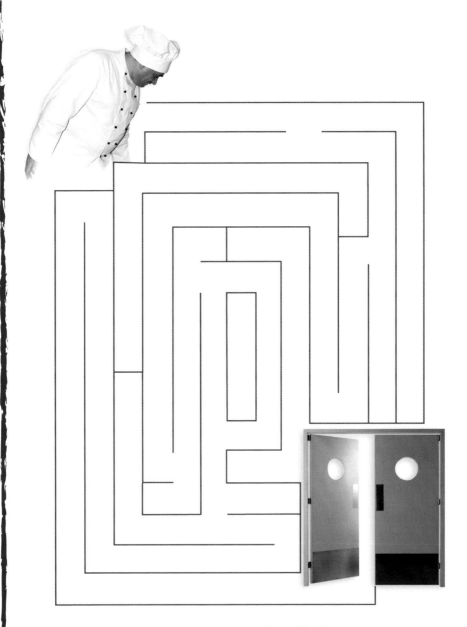

④ DESSERTS

My Favorite Chapter

This is the final chapter, *my favorite chapter,* all about dessert. I don't think a meal is complete without a tasty dessert. The first thing I ever made in the kitchen was chocolate chip cookies.

I have always loved baking. There is something so special about the smell of fresh baked bread, cookies, or cake. I remember staying home from school on snow days and gathering in the kitchen with my family to bake and stir up some fun memories. Those were fun and delicious days. I was fortunate to have snow days, but for those of you who live in a warmer climate, you can create your own snow day on a Saturday, Sunday, or another day when you have no school by getting your family together to bake some of the recipes you find in this chapter.

Here you will learn the basics of baking and a couple of my secrets that make baking extra special. I find that making dessert is a great time to dig in, get creative, and have fun. There are no rules for having fun in the kitchen as long as you remember it is important to keep the kitchen clean and to clean up your mess.

I give you some of my most cherished recipes here, and I hope you enjoy them as much as I have.

—*Chef Antonio Frontera*

Baking School 101:
The Chemistry of Baking

What is the purpose of these ingredients?

Sugar: It gives a sweet flavor and browns food.

Liquid: Without liquid, baked food wouldn't stick together.

Flour: It's the building block of baked food. When liquid is added to it, it absorbs it, swells, and sticks together.

Fats: They make baked products tender by coating the wheat gluten and keeping it from developing.

Eggs: Like liquid, eggs make ingredients stick together. They also add flavor, richness, and a tender texture.

Leavening agent: A leavening agent is a substance that causes dough to rise.

Types of Sugar

• Granulated sugar is white, processed, and the type most commonly used.

• Powdered sugar is less sweet, finer than granulated, and used in most icings.

• Brown sugar is less processed, more flavorful, and mostly used in cookies.

• Splenda is a no-calorie sweetener.

Never, Too Messy

I'd begun to regret my promise that no activity was too messy. I wanted our three-year-old to know that I cared about him more than any mess, so usually there were no limits when we did crafts, or painting, or baking.

As we were making Grandpa's birthday cake, Dante stood on the step stool that had belonged to Great Grandma Fritz. I loved recalling her perched on its seat in her kitchen when I was his age, her feet resting on the two steps. Now Dante stood on the top step so he could see to crack the eggs into the bowl. As I picked remnants of shell from the batter, he added the cup of sugar, which I wiped from the counter back into the bowl. Rigorously, his little hand stirred and stirred as I slowly added the first cup of flour. The dough stiffened. He stirred harder. Suddenly he tumbled off the bottom step and onto the floor, knocking the five-pound bag of flour over himself, the stool, my feet, and the entire kitchen floor.

I gasped at the sight!

He quickly jumped up and blinked flour from his eyelashes. "I'm okay, Mom. I'm okay."

—Angela Thieman Dino

What did
the egg do when
it heard a joke?

It cracked up!

#6 COOKIES STRAIGHT FROM THE OVEN —

These taste at least ten thousand times better than the cookies you buy at the store. Maybe the smell of chocolate chip cookies in the oven is the way heaven smells. And when that oven door opens and those cookies come out, still huffing and puffing with heat, that's the moment to sniff the delicious aroma. Wait until the pan cools a bit, and put that first cookie in your mouth. The little chocolate chips are still soft enough to melt on your tongue. The cookie edges are crisp. The milk you drink with it is icy cold. One is never enough— especially not for Grandpa!

"The Kitchen is *my* canvas."

CUTOUT COOKIES

MAKES 3 DOZEN
CAN VARY DEPENDING UPON SIZE OF CUTTER.

C is for cookie; that's good enough for me.

—Cookie Monster

INGREDIENTS

- 1 cup (2 sticks) butter, softened
- 1½ cups white sugar
- 2 eggs
- 1 teaspoon vanilla extract
- 1 teaspoon lemon extract
- 2 cups all-purpose flour
- 1 teaspoon baking powder
- 1 pinch salt
- Additional flour for rolling out the dough
- Icing and sprinkles

TOOLS

2 large mixing bowls

Electric hand mixer

Measuring cups

Measuring spoons

Rolling pin

Cookie cutters

Cookie sheet pans

Cooling racks

> 💡 **TIP:**
> You can freeze leftover dough and take it out as needed to bake fresh cookies!

Directions

1 **Preheat** the oven to 350 degrees.

2 **In** one of the large bowls, beat together the butter and sugar with the mixer until fluffy.

3 **Beat** in the eggs one at a time. Then stir in the vanilla and lemon extracts.

4 **In** a separate bowl, combine the flour, baking powder, and salt. Gradually blend in the butter and sugar mixture to form a soft dough. Cover the dough with plastic wrap and refrigerate it overnight.

5 **On** a floured surface, roll out a ¼-inch-thick sheet of dough.

6 **Cut** the dough into desired shapes using the cookie cutters.

7 **Place** cookies 2 inches apart on ungreased cookie sheet pans.

8 **Bake** for 10 minutes, or until lightly browned, then cool on the wire racks.

9 **Decorate** with icing and sprinkles.

S'MORES

INGREDIENTS

- 2 graham crackers
- 1 marshmallow
- 1 piece (½ piece of chocolate)

TOOLS

Microwave-safe dish

Microwave

MAKES 1 S'MORE

DIRECTIONS

1 SANDWICH an untoasted marshmallow and a piece of chocolate between 2 graham crackers.

2 PUT the "sandwich" on a microwave-safe dish.

3 MICROWAVE until the marsh-mallow is soft.

FUN FACT:
According to *The Guinness Book of World Records*, the largest s'more ever was made in 2003, weighed 1,600 pounds, and used 20,000 marshmallows.

BEATING THE SYSTEM

I can remember the precise moment when a family tradition began.

I was new at grandmothering, a bit overwhelmed, and three-year-old Hannah was having a classic meltdown. She had stayed overnight with her grandpa and me, and we were quickly running out of diversions. Suddenly, this tiny blond dynamo was staging a minor tantrum, related, I'm sure, to a severe case of homesickness.

What to do? I'd already run out of the traditional distractions: modified games of hide and seek, towers made of blocks, and finger painting. And there we were in the kitchen, fresh out of amusements.

Suddenly, as I opened the refrigerator to try soothing Hannah with some juice, inspiration hit. A row of eggs sat in their refrigerator nests—just plain old eggs.

I took one out and showed it to Hannah. She was unmoved. Then I promised her some "magic," and that got her attention. The tears stopped flowing.

My tools of the trade included one bowl, one primitive egg separator, and one ancient portable mixer.

Hannah, perched now on a stool, little feet dangling, was intrigued. *What was grandma going to do with this weird array of objects?*

She would soon find out.

I broke the egg and then separated the egg yolk from the white, praying I'd be successful. The ham in me emerged as I performed the delicate "surgery" with a flourish. My audience of one—Hannah—was duly impressed.

Then I showed Hannah the gloppy egg white in the bowl, an unimpressive sight.

Warmed up now, I might have been a ringleader at a major circus as I rolled up my sleeves, plugged in the portable mixer, and promised Hannah a kitchen version of the Greatest Show on Earth.

This little girl who had been so desolate minutes before watched with utter fascination. The egg white took on a life of its own as the blades of the mixer made it thicker and thicker until we had little, white mountains. Hannah actually cheered when I showed her the peaks.

"Again!" she demanded imperiously.

Three eggs later, she'd finally tired of the sport. But from that day on, making mountains out of egg whites became a highlight—dare I say a "peak experience"—of nearly every one of our visits.

Six more grandchildren have been born into a world of dazzling, battery-operated, and high-tech toys. Among them are four fierce little boys who seem destined to be whirling dervishes.

But each and every grandchild, boys included, has shared the egg white magic with Grandma, and each one has asked for more, more, more. I've even learned to salvage those stiffened egg whites and coax them into strange but interesting omelets.

This simplest of pleasures has been delightfully gratifying for this grandma.

I've flunked electronic games. I'm not much at building with geometric forms. But I whip up wicked egg whites and do a pretty decent narration for the three-year-old set. And I'd like to believe that in each of my grandchildren's memory banks there resides a gentle awakening to the wonders of the simply incredible egg.

Hannah, now a willowy twelve-year-old, recently kept me company in the kitchen before a family dinner, expertly arranging platters and putting the finishing touches on the salad. "Remember when we did the egg whites?" she asked as we worked side by side.

I glanced at this granddaughter with whom I had shared what most people would regard as far more important experiences since. Her sweet face was bathed in reverie, and a little smile played on her lips.

"Yes, I remember," I told Hannah.

But I couldn't begin to tell her just how warmly and well.

—Sally Friedman

A. BACALL

"I never actually knew cooking was such a violent activity. You have to beat the eggs, whip the cream and mash the nuts."

MERINGUE COOKIES

🛒 INGREDIENTS

- 4 egg whites
- ½ teaspoon cream of tartar
- 3 tablespoons dry skim milk powder
- ⅔ cup sugar
- 2 teaspoons vanilla extract

🍴 TOOLS

Mixing bowl

Electric hand mixer

Measuring spoons

Baking sheet pan

Parchment paper

Tablespoon

👆 VARIATION:
To vary the flavor, add ½ teaspoon of mint extract when you add the vanilla.

MAKES 7 DOZEN

164

DIRECTIONS

1 PREHEAT the oven to 300 degrees.

2 BEAT the egg whites with the mixer until foamy. Add the cream of tartar and beat until fluffy but not stiff. Add the skim milk powder, vanilla extract, and sugar gradually, and mix well. Continue beating until all the sugar is dissolved and the meringue is stiff.

3 LINE the baking sheet pan with parchment paper. Drop cookies by the tablespoonful onto the paper.

4 BAKE for 40 to 45 minutes.

🍎 HEALTH TIP:
Eat snacks and other foods made with egg whites rather than whole eggs.

💡 TIP:
You can add food coloring befitting the holiday or celebration of your choice. Mix and match colors, and have fun!

GRaNDPa JOE'S JELLY COOKiES

My grandfather created this recipe. He passed it down to my parents, who passed it down to me. It is very special to my family, and these are myfavorite cookies ever. Now I tell my father that I make the best, but he still insists he does!

USE YOUR hANDS a LOT iN THiS RECiPE. DON'T BE SHY!

INGREDiENTS

- 2 cups (4 sticks) butter
- (1 stick) margarine
- 1½ cups sugar
- 5 to 6 cups all-purpose flour
- 1 jar (16 ounces) grape jelly

TOOLS

12 x 16-inch baking sheet pan

Diamond-shaped cookie cutters

2 mixing bowls

Measuring cups

Fork

Cooling rack

DIRECTIONS

MAKES
3 DOZEN
CAN VARY DEPENDING
ON SIZE OF COOKIE
CUTTER,

1 **PREHEAT** the oven to 350 degrees.

2 **IN** the mixing bowl, soften the butter and margarine with your hands.

3 **ADD** the sugar to the butter and margarine and mix thoroughly until smooth.

Directions *(continued)*

4 **GRADUALLY** add the flour,
1 cup at a time, stirring with your
hands until all is incorporated.
Keep adding flour until the dough
is firm but not sticky.

5 **TAKE** half the dough and
pat it smoothly and evenly
into the 12 x 16-inch baking
sheet pan.

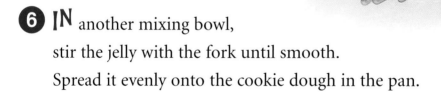

6 **IN** another mixing bowl,
stir the jelly with the fork until smooth.
Spread it evenly onto the cookie dough in the pan.

7 **ROLL** the other half of the dough into ropes. Place
criss-cross onto the jelly until you run out of dough.

8 **BAKE** for 35 to 45 minutes.

9 **COOL** on a rack and then cut the cookies into
diamond shapes.

LiTTLe MaN CoDy COOKiES

"What's that, Grandma?" asked my three-year old grandson, Cody.

I slipped my faded, stained apron over my head and adjusted it. "An apron."

Cody looked puzzled. "Why?"

I remembered his mother didn't bother with aprons. "I wear it to keep my clothes clean. Sometimes cooking gets messy."

I could see this idea entering his mind. "Okay."

I stepped into the pantry to collect the ingredients. "Cody, you will love these yummy chocolate cookies we're going to make. I'll read the recipe to you. Since you're such a good counter, you can add the things we need into my big bowl. I'll do the hot part, and you can do some of the stirring."

I gathered sugar, baking cocoa, quick-cooking oats, peanut butter, and vanilla and put them on the counter. As I took the milk and butter from the refrigerator, I could hear Cody scooting my kitchen stool toward the counter. I knew my budding chef was ready.

"I keep my clothes clean, too," Cody announced.

I turned around to look at my grandson. On the floor was a pile of his clothes. Standing on my kitchen stool was a completely naked child.

We made our cookies and both of us kept our clothes clean. Since that day, however, every time we have made chocolate oatmeal cookies, we remember our little man, Cody, standing naked in the kitchen.

—*Sharon L. Landeen*

Chocolate-Covered Raisin Haystacks

🛒 Ingredients

- 2 cups chocolate chips
- 1 can (4 ounces) sweetened condensed milk
- 2 cups mini–pretzel sticks, broken into pieces
- ½ cup raisins
- 1 cup peanuts

🏺 Tools

Measuring cups

Microwave-safe bowl

Microwave

Stirring spoon

Large mixing bowl

Baking sheet pan

Wax paper

Tablespoon

MAKES 3 DOZEN

Directions

MUNCH AND CRUNCH!

1 PLACE the chocolate chips and condensed milk in the microwave-safe bowl.

2 MICROWAVE on high in 10-second increments, stirring occasionally, until all chips and condensed milk are heated and smooth.

3 IN another large mixing bowl, break up the pretzels. Pour the chocolate mixture over the pretzels and stir. Add the raisins and peanuts and stir until completely coated.

4 LINE a baking sheet pan with wax paper. Drop the mixture onto the paper by the tablespoon. Chill for 3 hours.

You can easily find the PRETZELS in these haystacks!

Milk, and Cookies

My parents were creative in the kitchen, and they loved to putter with recipes and concoctions. I would climb up on a step stool so my parents and I could be side by side, and I would help them by stirring and blending. My dad always told me that the secret to cooking was "to add a little of this and a little of that." We would taste and change everything until it was just right.

I learned a lot in that kitchen, like that cookies would always bake differently. Sometimes the bottoms would get dark even if they were left in the oven just a second too long. So I learned how to check the clock and to use a timer.

I learned that sometimes recipes call for greasing pans, while other recipes don't. Directions or not, one time I got yucky shortening all over me. Another time, I could have been a character in a humorous cartoon, because flour was indeed flying—everywhere! It powdered my nose and speckled my dark brown hair. Flour even covered Muffin, our black cocker spaniel, who was at my feet observing and hoping for a taste.

My family had some rules, though: I couldn't turn on the oven, and I couldn't put anything in it without supervision. Because of these rules, I never felt completely independent. I really wanted the independence of saying, "I made it myself."

And then, one day something happened! A friend gave me a recipe I could "cook" all by myself. It was called "No-Cook Cookies." My parents said it was "kid-friendly." My dream came true. I could still be my mommy's (and daddy's) little helper in the kitchen *and* I could cook by myself! This recipe was perfect because all I had to do was mash vanilla wafers and mix and mix. My parents always told me that nothing needs to be perfect when you're cooking, as long as you do things carefully and safely. The cookie-batter balls that I rolled didn't have to be this way or that. Any size or shape would do, as long as they were left in the refrigerator long enough to chill.

I cannot tell you how many no-bake cookies I made in any batch. They were always different because I couldn't ever wait to lick the bowl. I even had an ever-changing recipe. Sometimes I tasted the bananas, supposedly to see if they were mushy or not.

How special and important I felt to finally "cook" by myself. That was an easy "recipe" for self-confidence, too. As my parents taught me, there is no right or wrong in the kitchen if you are careful and safe.

—*Gail Small*

"I ran out of sugar, so I used salt."

Chocolate Oatmeal Cookies

Y ummy, yummy in *your tummy!*
These are no-bake, quick and easy cookies.

Makes 3 Dozen

 Ingredients

- 2 cups white sugar
- ½ cup milk
- 1 tablespoon baking cocoa
- ½ cup peanut butter
- 8 tablespoons (1 stick) butter or margarine
- ½ teaspoon vanilla
- 3 cups quick-cooking oats

Tools

Measuring spoons

Measuring cups

Saucepan

Mixing spoon

Waxed paper

Tablespoon

Did you hear the joke about oatmeal?

It's a lot of mush.

DIRECTIONS

1 **COMBINE** the sugar, milk, cocoa, peanut butter and margarine or butter inthe saucepan. Bring the mixture to a boil while stirring. Boil for 1 minute.

2 **ADD** the vanilla and oats and stir well.

3 **DROP** cookies by the tablespoon onto waxed paper. Let them cool until firm.

The Spice of Life

I couldn't wait to show off my grandparents' home at Christmastime. I was sure my two best school friends had never before seen anything like it.

The neighbor's neatly shoveled yards looked bare and cold compared to ours. My grandfather piled the snow into minimoguls, like a dragon's back, for toboggan rides. The neighbors strangled their trees with electric lights, but my grandmother and I hung nuts and seed balls on our evergreens for the birds and squirrels. In my nine-year-old mind, our yard looked like a snow-globe village.

With a week to go before Christmas, Grandma Marya was up to her elbows in flour. She used to complain that her hands were stiffening with arthritis, but when she baked, knit sweaters for me, or tended wounded animals, her hands moved as quickly and lightly as butterflies. My grandmother was the storyteller, and she spoke through her hands. They had a lot to say at Christmas.

Our holiday preparations were as vast and elaborate as toy making in Santa's workshop. The kitchen was the headquarters of the operation. Marya and I would work at an enormous wood table, peeling, paring, and mixing, while my grandpa dropped in for taste tests. The kitchen table was my foundation in life; it was where I did homework, laid bare heartaches, and shared laughter.

This year I wanted to share my Christmas joy and fun with Janet and Gail, my two school friends. Janet and Gail floated in realms unfamiliar to me. They seemed to have a different dress for every day of the week.

They ate out in restaurants, too. What raised them to the level of the supernatural for me was their ability to make exquisite drawings that drew praise from the teacher. I considered myself lucky just to be able to associate with the artists.

The night before their arrival, I was aflutter with anxiety. I knew Janet liked apricots, so my grandma made apricot–walnut *kolachke,* which are Polish cookies. She had to keep a close eye on me to make sure that the cream cheese went into the dough and not into my mouth. Then there was the dark temptation of *makowiec,* a pastry that oozed an exotic, velvety, poppy-seed paste. I thought Gail would like that. The centerpiece was the *piernik,* or honey cake. My grandmother and I were up until midnight fussing over the confections.

My friends arrived after lunch the next day. My plan was to serve them tea and dessert and then surprise them with the chance to bake cookies with Grandma and me. When Janet and Gail cleared off their plates—more than once—I was relieved. My grandma also looked satisfied and rose to put on a kettle for more tea. She lifted the round lid on our cast-iron stove and tossed a hunk of wood inside. When a hungry flame leapt upward, Gail screamed and jumped back from the table.

"Isn't that dangerous?" asked Gail, her eyes fixed on the iron monster.

"No, it's better than an electric stove," I explained. "When I fell in the slush, my grandma dried my clothes near it, and I sat in front of it wrapped in a blanket. You can't do that with a regular stove."

"Don't you have a dryer?" Janet asked, aghast.

"Linda," my grandma interrupted, "can you go downstairs and get some potatoes for tonight's supper? I'll clear the table."

"Come see the basement," I suggested to my friends. "Blackbeard the cat is probably hiding down there." I reached for the flashlight above the door, but no one was following me down the stairs.

"Aren't you scared?" asked Gail. "You don't even have the proper electric light down there."

"The potatoes don't need light," I laughed. "Anyway, it reminds me of a Nancy Drew mystery. I pretend I'm exploring the cellar of a castle."

Apparently, my friends weren't big Nancy Drew fans. They stayed upstairs. When I came back up with an armful of potatoes, I saw that Grandma had set out the flour, spices, and cookie cutters. She held out two lacy aprons to my friends, who exchanged perplexed looks.

"So you don't get flour on your pretty clothes," I explained. "We're going to make gingerbread cookies."

"Oh, no!" said Janet, abruptly. "I forgot, I was supposed to call my mother."

I took her down the hallway and showed her the phone. As I walked away, I caught snippets of her conversation.

"No, Mother, I don't want to stay a moment longer. They're making us cook! And you should see their house! They're so poor, it's scary. They don't have a stove either. And they have to make all their own decorations. . . . Yes, right away. . . . Can you pick up Gail, too, Mother?"

My face and eyes burned, and I ran back down the hallway to the comfort of the kitchen. Janet reappeared, sounding very chipper.

"I forgot that I was supposed to go dress shopping with my mother, Linda. I'm really very sorry. We have a party tomorrow. My mom says she can drop you off, too, Gail."

Gail didn't need coaxing, and when the door closed on the two of them, I burst into tears.

"They didn't like anything," I wailed. "They said we were poor and didn't even have a normal house."

Grandma smoothed my hair, wiped my tears, and sat me down at the table in front of our cookie-making supplies. And we made cookies. After a while Grandma said, "We may not have as much as some of your friends, but it's not how much you have that's important. It's how much you do with what you have, and we do a lot. We have cookies and honey cake—simple things, simple ingredients. Maybe someday Janet and Gail will find the simple ingredients that make life special. Let's hope so."

"I hope so, Grandma," I said, smiling now.

—*Linda S. Handiak*

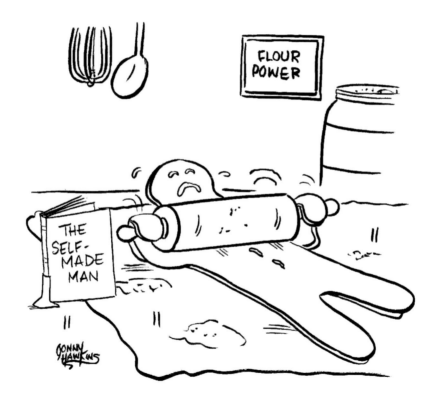

Gingerbread Man Workouts

Piernik (Honey Cake)

S uch sweet simplicity! When simple ingredients come together, amazing things can happen!

MAKES 4 LOAVES

🛒 INGREDIENTS

- Butter or vegetable oil for greasing the loaf pans
- 1 cup sugar
- 1 teaspoon ground cinnamon
- ½ teaspoon ground nutmeg
- ½ teaspoon ground cloves
- 4 eggs
- 1 cup canola oil
- 1 teaspoon baking soda
- 1 cup honey
- 4 cups all-purpose flour
- 1 tablespoon grated orange rind
- ½ cup chopped walnuts
- 1 cup strawberry jam

🏺 TOOLS

4 loaf pans

Measuring cups

Measuring spoons

Large bowl

Mixing spoon

Saucepan

Toothpick

Directions

1 **Preheat** the oven to 350 degrees.

2 **Grease** the 4 loaf pans.

3 **Mix** the sugar, cinnamon, nutmeg, cloves, and eggs in a large bowl. Stir in the oil and baking soda.

4 **Pour** the honey into a saucepan and bring it to a boil on medium heat. Then stir it into the egg mixture.

5 **Add** the flour, orange rind, and walnuts to the mixture. Stir for a few minutes, and then let the dough sit for an hour.

6 **Fill** each pan about halfway. Bake for 50 minutes or until a toothpick inserted into the center comes out clean. The top will be brown and cracked.

7 **Allow** the cake to cool a bit, then spread the strawberry jam over the top.

This cake makes a great gift!

FOR THE LOVE OF FUDGE

When I was growing up we went to Myrtle Beach in South Carolina every year, and we stayed for two long, delicious weeks. One of my favorite pastimes there was to visit the candy shops—the heady, sweet-smelling, decadent candy shops. There, spread out before the eye and nose was fudge galore, fudge of all flavors—vanilla and chocolate and butterscotch and a variety of other new, unique flavors. The fudge sat waiting behind a glass case, waiting for someone to ask for a sample, waiting for me.

Every year Mom would take me to buy a whole half pound. My favorite was cookies-and-crème fudge. Ah, cookies-and-crème! We sat on a bench on the boardwalk, and I would reach into my bag, break off a chunk, place it on my tongue, and let it melt, savoring every bit of that creamy mixture.

When we returned home, all I was left with were memories. So one year when I was in my teens, I complained to my mom that it wasn't fair to have cookies-and-crème fudge only once a year. Couldn't we have it during winter, too? Or whenever the craving hit us? My mom understood my fascination with fudge, for it was her love of fudge that got us into the groove of summer candy-shop hopping.

I thought she might say that she would look into ordering the fudge and having it shipped to our house. Perhaps once a month. But Mom surprised me by saying, "Let's try making that cookies-and crème fudge ourselves!"

I was amazed that she thought we could concoct anything as sublime as fudge from the beach shops. But mom always made chocolate fudge at Christmastime, and whenever we traveled she tested the local fudge, so she knew about making fudge.

That year Mom and I experimented, and, as it turned out, with a few creative alterations to her usual recipe we came up with amazing cookies-and-crème fudge that became one of our family traditions.

My mom passed away a few years ago, but I have continued her tradition of making fudge. I have her cookies-and-crème recipe, handwritten, framed, and hanging in a prominent spot in my kitchen. Each time I make her cookies-and-crème fudge for my family, standing over the stove and stirring dreamily, I remember Mom and her love of fudge.

—Tessa L. Floehr

COOKIES 'N CRÉME FUDGE

F udge is like family—sweet, lovable, and all-around wonderful.
I hope you enjoy making this treat with your family!

 INGREDIENTS

- 3 cups sugar

- ¾ cup (1½ sticks) butter
  or margarine

- 5 ounces evaporated milk

- 1 package (12 ounces)
  white chocolate chip morsels

- 1 jar (7 ounces)
  marshmallow cream

- 1 teaspoon vanilla
  extract

- 15 Oreo cookies,
  crushed

- Butter or
  vegetable oil for
  greasing the pan

TOOLS

Measuring cups

Measuring spoons

2½-quart saucepan

Mixing spoon

9 x 13-inch pan

Rolling pin

DIRECTIONS

1 **COMBINE** the sugar, butter or margarine, and evaporated milk in a heavy 2½-quart saucepan.

2 **BRING** the mixture to a full, rolling boil, stirring constantly.

MAKES
3 POUNDS

3 **ON** medium heat, continue boiling for 5 minutes, stirring constantly to prevent scorching.

4 **REMOVE** the saucepan from the heat. Stir in the white chocolate chips until melted. Add the marshmallow cream, vanilla, and crushed cookies. Beat with the mixing spoon until well blended.

5 **GREASE** the 9 x 13-inch pan and pour in the batter.

6 **SPRINKLE** with additional crushed cookies, if desired.

7 **COOL** at room temperature. Cut into squares.

Zizi Tina's Fudge

 INGREDIENTS

- ¾ cup margarine
- 3 cups sugar
- 5 ounces evaporated milk
- 12 ounces semisweet chocolate chips
- Butter or vegetable oil for greasing the pan
- 7 ounces marshmallow cream

TOOLS

Measuring cups

Microwave-safe bowl

Microwave

9 x 13-inch baking pan

Mixing spoon

DIRECTIONS

1 GREASE the 9 x 13-inch baking pan.

2 MICROWAVE the margarine on high in a large microwave-safe bowl for approximately 1 minute, or until melted.

MAKES 3 POUNDS

3 ADD the sugar and evaporated milk.

4 MICROWAVE the mixture on high for approximately 5 minutes, or until the mixture begins to boil.

5 ADD the chocolate chips to the mixture and stir until the chips are melted. Add the marshmallow cream and mix well. Pour the mixture into the baking pan.

6 COOL at room temperature and cut into squares.

Peanut Butter Pie

🛒 Ingredients

- 1 cup peanut butter
- 1 cup cream cheese
- ¼ cup confectioners' sugar
- 3 tablespoons milk
- 1 teaspoon vanilla extract
- 1 cup heavy cream
- 1 9-inch graham cracker crust
- 2 cups chocolate chips
- 2 tablespoons oil
- 1 cup sour cream

🧂 Tools

Measuring cups

Measuring spoons

2 mixing bowls

Electric mixer

Microwave-safe bowl

Microwave

Spatula

Nutty Fact:
George Washington Carver created 105 recipes using the peanut as a key ingredient!

Directions

Makes a 9-inch Pie

1 **IN** the mixing bowl, use an electric mixer to beat together the peanut butter, cream cheese, confectioners' sugar, milk, and vanilla.

2 **IN** another mixing bowl and with a clean mixer, beat the heavy cream until firm.

3 **FOLD** the whipped cream into the peanut butter mixture. Pour the mixture into the graham cracker crust. Refrigerate the pie until it's firm.

4 **IN** a microwave-safe bowl, melt the chocolate chips and oil on high, stirring every 30 seconds.

5 **REMOVE** the mixture from the microwave. Add the sour cream and stir until blended. Pour this mixture over the pie and spread it with the spatula. Chill until firm. Cut and serve.

Snow Ice Cream

I flattened my nose against the cold, damp windowpane to watch the swirling snowflakes. The spinning frenzy of icy crystals made me dizzy. Except for flashes of red and blue around the bird feeder, the rest of the world looked draped in marshmallow cream frosting.

The glass squeaked as I outlined a wobbly snowman in the beads of moisture dotting the windowpane.

A lime-green, 1950 Chevy crept toward the house. "Here comes Daddy," I yelled, bouncing off the sofa. I pressed my back against the side of the refrigerator, waiting. The door on the screened porch creaked open, and I could hear him stomping.

"Boo," I said, jumping out at him as the kitchen door swung open.

"What's going on here?" He set his black lunch bucket on the counter and lifted me into the air.

"Daddy, Daddy," I squealed, nuzzling my cheek against his whisker stubble and relishing his familiar scent of tobacco and a hint of Old Spice.

"It's a blizzard out there," he said before putting me down.

Mama came over and gave him a hug. "I'm glad you made it home safely." She turned toward the stove. "Time to wash your hands," she said, piling a bowl high with golden-brown, fried potatoes.

Daddy was scrubbing his hands at the kitchen sink, so I ran to the bathroom, dabbing some water on my hands with a tiny bit of soap.

"Mmmm, I'm hungry," Daddy said, scooting up to the square, wooden table. Plates were filled with golden corn, thick slices of ham, steaming potatoes, and iceberg lettuce salad.

"Mama's feeding us rabbit food again," Daddy teased, winking at me as he took a bite of salad.

We talked about our day and enjoyed the meal, finishing with chocolate pudding topped with Dream Whip.

Mama and I scraped the dishes. She washed and I dried, while Daddy settled in the living room with the newspaper. When the last dish was put away, Mama and I played Chinese checkers at the kitchen table. After a while, Daddy got up from the sofa and came into the kitchen to join us. He opened the bottom cabinet door, reached way back, and removed several pans.

I squatted down beside him. "Whatcha looking for?"

He pulled out a large, white enamel pan with a black rim. "I'm getting some snow. Want to come with me?" He took a big slotted spoon from the drawer.

"Snow?"

He grabbed his coat hanging by the door and went out onto the back porch to buckle on his overshoes. "Hurry and get your coat and boots."

"Why are we getting snow?"

"Come on. I'll show you."

I ran to the closet for my red, shiny boots. Before I had finished buttoning my coat and tying on my cap, Mama handed me a huge pair of yellow rubber gloves. "Put these on over your other gloves to keep your hands dry. And try not to get snow in your boots."

I followed Daddy out the back door into the winter stillness. The bright glow of the backyard surprised me. Snowflakes stung my face, and I stuck out my tongue to catch some.

"Come on, Hon. Let's go around front by the streetlight."

"Ooooh, I think I stepped in a snowdrift."

"This won't take long," he said. "Then you can put on dry socks."

Beneath the hazy glow of the streetlight, Daddy brushed the top of a snowdrift. He scooped up the clean snow underneath and piled it high in the bowl.

I was busy making a snowball.

"Come on, Linda. Let's hurry before this melts," he said.

We stomped our way to the back porch, leaving wet trails on the concrete. Mama had milk, sugar, and vanilla out on the kitchen counter. A metal beater whirred as she turned the handle, sending liquid sloshing inside a bowl.

"Quick, come and help me," she said. "Spoon in the snow."

I flung my coat on the hook and pulled my boots off on the rug. Clumps of snow fell from my socks. I slipped on my saddle oxfords before Mama noticed. With the big, slotted spoon, I added clumps of the frozen white stuff.

"Some people put eggs in their ice cream, but I can't stand the thought of raw eggs in my snow ice cream," she said.

"No, Mama." I shook my head. "I don't want any raw eggs either."

"Eat before it melts," she said, handing me a bowl of the creamy mixture.

Spoons clinked as we enjoyed the wonderful treat. It was much soupier than regular ice cream, but the taste made me wish for snow every day during wintertime.

—*Linda Perkins*

#7 **Mushy Ice Cream**—I'm not talking about the kind of ice cream that's hard as a rock when it comes out of the freezer, or the kind you can't dent with your spoon no matter how hard you try. Think about the ice cream that's been left out on the kitchen table, or maybe on the deck, melting in the summer sun. Think of it as the best, most delicious, kind of syrupy soup. Then take your spoon and scoop it up when it's not yet liquid but it's not still hard. That's the moment you have to seize it!

Make Your Own Ice Cream

Ingredients

- ½ cup plus ½ cup cold milk
- 1 envelope unflavored gelatin
- ¾ cup sugar
- ¼ teaspoon vanilla
- 2 cups heavy cream

Tools

Measuring cups

Mixing bowl

Microwave-safe bowl

Microwave

Measuring spoons

Electric hand mixer

Plastic wrap

Rubber or silicone spatula

Shallow cake pan

DiRECTiONS

① PoUR ½ cup of the cold milk into a mixing bowl. Sprinkle the gelatin over the milk. Let the mixture stand for 5 minutes. Heat the other ½ cup of milk in a microwave-safe bowl in a microwave until hot. Add the heated milk to the gelatin mix. Mix with an electric mixer for approximately 2 minutes until well blended.

② BEaT in the sugar and vanilla.

③ FREEZE the mixture. Periodically, take it out of the freezer and stir it.

SERVES a PaRTy OF 4–6

④ BEaT the heavy cream on high with an electric mixer until firm.

⑤ GENTLY fold the whipped cream into the gelatin mixture, using a rubber or silicone spatula.

⑥ PoUR the ice cream into a shallow cake pan and cover it with plastic wrap. Freeze the ice cream until it's hard.

The Best Part of The Game

"Remember to be a good sport," Dad said as he and Mommy walked me to the dugout to meet my team for warm-up.

"I wonder who's bringing snacks today," I said.

My dad stooped to look me in the eyes while he talked to me. Dad smiled. "Remember, it's not about winning. Just do your best for the team."

I said, "I hope it's Justin's mom. She brings the best snacks."

As I ran out to left field I heard Dad call out, "Keep your eye on the ball and your head in the game."

Usually I just picked dandelions out there because there was nothing else to do—*no six-year-old can hit a ball to left field!* I thought to myself.

Finally, two caterpillars and one ladybug later, the game was over and we all ran to the dugout—faster than we ran the bases—and snacks! Sure enough, Justin's mom brought Ding Dongs *and* soda pop. She always brought the best stuff. Most moms did. Except mine. Other moms brought cookies and candy all tied up in cool sacks or with fun strings. Mom said that the competition was getting to be more about snacks than sports. She said she wasn't going to play that game. *What game,* I wondered. *I thought we were playing baseball.*

Every time it was my turn for snacks, Mom brought simple stuff like Oreos and juice. My friends didn't seem very excited, and I didn't feel very special. I didn't say anything to Mom about her lousy snacks, because I didn't want her to feel bad, but inside I was disappointed.

One day it was almost 100 degrees in left field! But I didn't mind playing in the toughest heat. I stood out there, being a good sport, slamming my fist into the pocket of my glove, thinking about the popsicles Tommy's mom would bring. She'd have them wrapped in superhero napkins with matching ribbon. Presentation, Mom called it, shaking her head.

On the last game of the season, it was my turn to bring snacks. When Mom asked me what I wanted, I just said, "Whatever," in a grumbly voice.

Finally, the boring game was over (there were no butterflies, bugs, or baseballs in left field that day). My friends and I ran fast to the dugout, and there was Mom, holding the pretty picnic basket Grandma had given us. Inside were cool baseball napkins with matching plates—and ice cream bars!

As Mom handed out the snacks, my friend yelled, "Wow, Bailey! You brought the best snack ever!"

I couldn't help but smile.

My mom is such a good sport. As I grew up, I learned my mom knows how to play the "game" too.

—Bailey Corona
as told to LeAnn Thieman

Ice Cream Party

Thris is so much better than a tea party with kings and queens. It's an ice cream party you can share with your friends.

 **INGREDIENTS**

- 6 cups vanilla ice cream (It's more fun if you make the ice cream yourself!)

- Whipped cream

- Chocolate syrup

- Mix-ins (your choice): gummy bears, Oreo cookies, brownies, chocolate fudge, chocolate chips, peanut butter

 TOOLS

Marble pastry board

Pot holders, towel, or oven mitts

Metal baking scraper

Ice cream scoop

4 to 6 ice cream bowls

4 to 6 spoons

DIRECTIONS

1 CHILL the marble pastry board in a freezer for 2 hours. Remove it from the freezer using pot holders, a towel, or oven mitts, being careful not to freeze your hands.

2 PUT the ice cream on the board and add your choice of mix-ins.

SERVES
4-6

3 USE the metal baking scraper to cut into the ice cream. Twist and turn the ice cream so that it thoroughly blends with the mix-ins.

4 SCOOP the ice cream into bowls. Then decorate each serving with whipped cream and chocolate syrup.

ENJOY IT!

SOFT, SWEET MEMORIES

During the summer of 1962, when I was only six, I first learned how to cook. I didn't learn in the usual way, in the usual place. No, not with pots and pans and stirrers and spoons. No, not even in a kitchen. Nor was the first dish prepared by my own little hands a simple soup, or an omelet, or even a grilled-cheese sandwich. I learned to cook out in the Texas desert, not far from the slow-rolling, muddy Rio Grande, the border between the United States and Mexico. My witnesses were my family and a circle of coyotes, their yellow eyes aglow in the deep desert dark.

My mom and dad had been raising the four of us—my brother Larry, my sister Mani, me, and my baby sister, Patti—to be as self-sufficient as possible. They had finally taken us on a campout. This was the height of adventure for us. We didn't have the amenities people have now—no bulging, overstuffed RV, no starter matches, not even any logs for the fire. We didn't have a tent either. We roughed it with a crude canvas awning, set up circus style, with ropes and spikes and a big metal pole in the center.

We arrived at our campsite in late afternoon. After unloading, setting up our shelter, and gathering firewood, Dad allowed us to go for a swim in a nearby spring. Night fell suddenly, and we three older kids—all chilled—bundled into an old army blanket and sat around the campfire. Dad, an expert with fires, blended mesquite and pine logs into a crackling fragrant symphony. The fragrance and the sparks floated into the dark sky, joining the stars shining against the blackness of the night.

The warmth and bright dancing of the fire made me dreamy. After a while I realized my eyes were getting heavy. But I still had my bathing suit on and, although I was now warm, I was still uncomfortably damp. So I stood up, intending to change into my pajamas. Then I heard my dad's voice.

"Hold on. There's something I want to show you."

I sank back down onto the log we were all sitting on and watched my dad as he reached into a plastic bag stuffed with white, fluffy-looking shapes.

FUN FACT:

Marshmallow candy was first made by Egyptians over 3,000 years ago. The Egyptians made candy from the root of the marshmallow plant. Today, marshmallows do not contain any marshmallow root; gelatin is substituted for the sweet, sticky root.

"You are about to learn the secrets of making a perfectly roasted marshmallow!"

My mom came up to the fire then. She had just finished giving my baby sister a bath. She saw what Dad was doing, and she had a smile on her face. She sat next to me on the log and put her arm around me.

"You know, Terri, marshmallows come from a plant." She reached into the bag and drew out one of the white, fluffy shapes.

"You'll like these. Here. Taste."

I took the marshmallow and bit into it. We weren't often given candy of any kind, so the sweet taste combined with the soft texture came as close to heaven as I had ever known in my six years on Earth. "Delicious," I said as well as I could with a mouthful of the sweet stuff. My brother and older sister came to the fire then, already in their pajamas.

"Now," my father said to my brother and sister, "you two know how to do this already. So you stay put. This is Theresa's turn."

He held the stick with the marshmallow on the end as he lowered it over the campfire. "There's a secret to a perfectly roasted marshmallow," he said, and I could see the eyes of the coyotes as they rounded the campfire, to my relief too shy to approach the fire but hungry enough to come close, hoping for an easy snack. Dad lowered the stick so the marshmallow hung just over the flames; the white outside turned golden as he turned the stick. "You don't hold it too close to the fire," he said, continuing the lesson. "If you do, it'll burn and maybe fall off. Hold it near the fire, and turn it so it roasts all over. Then, after a few seconds, you let it catch fire," and as he said this, the marshmallow began to flame. "Then you bring it close and blow it out." He held the flaming delicacy near my face, and I blew until the marshmallow's flame died.

Then I reached for my marshmallow.

"No, no," said Dad. "You have to wait till it cools, or else you'll burn your tongue. Waiting is the hardest part for me, too."

I leaned my chin on my hand and gazed at the molten marshmallow, my taste buds tingling, and then at the campfire still dancing and crackling, and then at the hungry circle of coyote eyes glowing in the vast, velvety night.

As I watched and waited, my brother and sister took sticks and began roasting their marshmallows.

"Now it's your turn, Teresa," Dad said as he handed me a mesquite stick.

Carefully, determined to succeed, I threaded my very own marshmallow onto the stick, shook it to be sure it was on tight, and then brought it to the fire and lowered it over the flames.

"Yes, that's right," Dad said, encouragingly. "Just another second then."

Suddenly the marshmallow caught fire, and a rainbow of colors shot into the night.

"Now blow it out!"

I don't know where the thought came from, but I thought it was a pretty smart thought. Why bother blowing the flame out? Why not just wave the stick and let the night put it out?

"No, don't do that—" was all my father could get out before my still-flaming marshmallow, like a bird, flew off my stick, over and past the campfire and the heads of my brother and sister, and into the deep dark. The coyotes growled and snarled as they fought for the morsel. They squealed and they howled as their tongues got the burn of sweet surprise.

I was embarrassed and brokenhearted, and tears leaked out of the corners of my eyes.

"That's all right," my Dad said cheerfully. "You'll do better next time."

And I did of course. I got better and better at it.

To this day I remember the taste of those marshmallows I roasted out there in the Texas desert: the sweet, caramelized semiburnt outside, the soft, gooey inside.

It's not so easy to cook a perfectly roasted marshmallow. Just recently I gave my own two kids their first lesson in cooking—not in a kitchen but around a campfire in the Texas desert.

—T. Jensen Lacey

HOMEMADE MARSHMALLOWS

MAKES APPROX. 2 DOZEN

In my youth, my family would go on fishing trips, camp out, and toast marshmallows over the open fire. Cooking with my family was comfort to my soul. We loved popping these marshmallows into our mouths!

 ## INGREDIENTS

- 3 envelopes unflavored gelatin
- ½ cup plus 2 tablespoons water
- 2 cups granulated sugar
- Butter or vegetable oil for greasing the pan
- 1 teaspoon vanilla
- 1 cup confectioners' sugar

 ## TOOLS

Small bowl

Measuring cups

Measuring spoons

Medium saucepan

Mixing bowl

Electric mixer

9 x 13-inch baking pan

#8 MARSHMALLOWS—Aren't marshmallows silly? Aren't they like chubby little clouds that make you want to mush them up and play with them even before you pop them in your mouth? Grandpa and I love to toast marshmallows. Once you take your first bite, can you ever stop eating a marshmallow? Nope!

Directions

1 **IN** a small bowl, stir together the gelatin and ½ cup of water. Add another 2 tablespoons of water. Set aside.

2 **IN** a medium saucepan, combine the granulated sugar and ½ cup of water. Add another 2 tablespoons of water and the vanilla. Heat the mixture on low heat. Stir until the sugar is dissolved. Cook sugar until candy thermo-meter reaches 240 degrees. Slowly add mix-ture to gelatin while beating with mixer.

3 **Beat** with an electric mixer until it's foamy and thick—approximately 15 minutes.

4 **Lightly** dust a 9 x 13-inch baking pan with confectioners sugar.

5 **Pour** the gelatin sugar mixture into the baking pan and dust with confectioners' sugar, and let it set overnight on the counter top, uncovered.

The Honey-Apple Pie Cure

Everyone in our little town of five hundred knew enough to keep away from Mr. Wendell, but dad still bought the house right next door! I was eleven, unwillingly carting boxes in while fearing the scowling old man watching and picking apples from the trees beside the tall wire-fenced wall that separated our yards.

All the children in the town were afraid of him and called him Mr. Nasty because he put a big sign on his door that said "Go Away!"

I think, even the grown-ups didn't like Mr. Wendell, because one day in the store, I overheard Mrs. Weaver complaining about him. My mom replied, "Hurting people hurts others." All afternoon I wondered how Mr. Wendell got hurt and how it helped for him to hurt others. It was a riddle that had me worrying if he would hurt Dad as he approached the fence to introduce himself. But Mr. Wendell just yelled, "Keep away. Don't you dare take apples from my tree." I thought, *What a welcome!*

A year later, I still trembled at the memory of that unfriendly greeting and kept my distance from the fence. But one day, I reasoned to myself that any apples that had fallen in our yard from a branch hanging over that fence were fair game. Boy, was I wrong! Mr. Wendell came out just as I had picked up my fifth apple, yelling, "Stop thief." There I stood, frozen in fear, until Mom came to the door and he finally removed himself, and his red face, from my view, releasing my feet to run safely into the house.

Dad was home for lunch, just in time to listen to me sob my story to Mom, vengefully wishing ill on our nasty neighbor. "You catch more bees with honey than vinegar," Dad said.

Mom smiled in that *I've-got-a-secret* way and said, "I think we'll just give Mr. Wendell his apples back." I worried about the "we" until she pulled out the honey and frozen piecrusts from the freezer. Honey–apple pie. Yum! I tried to forget Mr. Wendell as Mom let me mix the streusel and measure out the spices while she peeled the apples and mixed them with the spices and honey. I held the brown paper bag while mom slipped in the finished pie to bake while we started dinner.

I hid behind my mom like a baby when she rang Mr. Nasty's doorbell. He looked as if he could chew nails, and I couldn't manage to speak. So, she nodded at me and said, "Delores made this honey–apple pie from the dropped apples." He stared for a second, then grabbed the pie and pushed the door shut with his foot.

Dad told us at dinner that we'd done the right thing. I wasn't so sure until an hour later, when the doorbell rang, and Mom answered the door. There stood Mr. Wendell holding a basket of apples! I backed to the safety of the dining room doorway. He cleared his throat and looked around the room until his eyes latched on to me, and he whispered, "Girlie, I'm sorry. I've been such a grouch. I haven't had pie like that since Edith passed on."

"Uh," he stuttered, "you can take all the apples you want from my trees—but only you. Don't you go bringin' a bunch of rascals with you."

I felt tears sting my eyes and couldn't answer, so I just stood there and nodded. He turned around and rushed off toward his house. I stood still for a minute.

Then we all smiled as Dad chuckled, his mouth full of some of his second piece of honey–apple pie. "Good job," he said. "Glad you made two pies." While licking the sticky syrup off his lips, he added thoughtfully, "Honey is a healer, you know, and I think your pie might just have begun healing a broken heart."

—*Delores Liesner*

ANTONIO'S BROWNIES

These are my ultimate brownies. I whipped up this recipe when I was a young lad using leftover ingredients my mom had in the cupboards. *Voilà! Like magic!*

🛒 INGREDIENTS

- Butter and flour for greasing the pan
- 6 tablespoons (¾ stick) butter
- ½ cup flour
- 4 ounces semisweet chocolate
- ¾ cup sugar
- 1 tablespoon vanilla
- 2 eggs
- 1½ teaspoons salt
- 10 ounces unsweetened cocoa powder
- 1½ cups semisweet chocolate chips
- ½ cup white chocolate chips
- ¼ cup Reese's Pieces
- ½ cup chopped maraschino cherries
- Butterscotch syrup

TOOLS

8-inch square baking pan

Microwave-safe bowl

Microwave

Measuring cups

Measuring spoons

Small microwave-safe bowl

Electric mixer

Toothpick

Cooling rack

DIRECTIONS

MAKES
9
BROWNIES

1 PREHEAT the oven to 350 degrees.

2 BUTTER, and flour an 8-inch square baking pan.

3 IN a microwave-safe bowl, melt the chocolate on medium, stirring occasionally. Heat in 30-second increments until melted.

4 ADD the butter. Then, add the sugar and vanilla. Beat with the electric hand mixer until smooth.

5 FOLD in the eggs, salt, cocoa powder, flour, semisweet chocolate chips, white chocolate chips, Reese's Pieces, and cherries.

6 SPREAD the batter in the prepared pan and bake for 25 to 35 minutes.

7 INSERT a toothpick in the center to test for doneness. If it's dry and crumby, it's done. If not, continue cooking.

8 COOL on a cooling rack. Drizzle with a little butterscotch syrup and serve.

FEED THEM AND THEY WILL COME

Every afternoon, my daughter Lauren moves from the crowded halls of a busy high school to the manic parking lot that resembles the bumper cars at the fair, to her final destination: our relatively tranquil kitchen. To ease the transition, I like to surprise her with one of her favorite snacks, cucumber sandwiches and tea.

I introduced Lauren to cucumber sandwiches as a result of my love for tea and tea food. Teatime after school is the perfect opportunity to share our day and to catch up on all the important things going on in my daughter's life. As we discuss everything from what she ate for lunch to which boy she is currently attracted to, our break gives us time to connect at an age when communication often breaks down.

My college-age son, Timothy, enjoys tea for breakfast. Each morning, I arise first and put the kettle on. The shrill whistle of the kettle as the water comes to a boil acts as his alarm clock. Our day begins together as we share a cup of tea.

Food is a natural draw for teenagers. I've found the secret to attracting my children's friends to our home involves an easy recipe: Mix one large bowl of seasonally colored M&M's with a baked goodie, such as brownies or cookies. Add an occasional quick meal, and I'm serving a crowd before the oven has cooled. While stuffing their mouths they talk (while chewing, of course), and I scarf up information as quickly as a dog ravishes food dropped to the floor. Laughter, tears, and insight into what makes these aliens called teenagers tick can be found underneath a grilled-cheese sandwich. Feed them and they will come.

As a result of this bonding over food, I have many adopted children. Our neighbor's son, Kenny, calls me "Mom." I consider it an honor.

And so I feed them, and I learn as I laugh and cry and realize that all too soon my table will be empty and my pantry way too full.

I think it's time to make some more brownies.

—Jo Rae Cash

"I'll probably do better when I learn to read."

Reprinted by permission of Bruce Robinson. ©2007 Bruce Robinson.

APPLE BROWNIES

I even put apples in my brownies because, as the old saying goes, "An apple a day keeps the doctor away."

MAKES 12 BROWNIES

🛒 INGREDIENTS

- 12 tablespoons (1½ sticks) butter
- 1½ cups sugar
- 2 eggs
- 2 cups peeled and grated apples
- 2 cups all-purpose flour
- 1 teaspoon baking soda
- 1 teaspoon baking powder
- 1 teaspoon salt
- 1 teaspoon ground cinnamon
- Butter or vegetable oil for greasing the pan

🏺 TOOLS

Grater

Measuring spoons

Measuring cups

Mixing bowl

Electric mixer

9 x 13-inch baking pan

Toothpick

DIRECTIONS

1 PREHEAT the oven to 350 degrees.

2 IN a mixing bowl, cream the butter with an electric mixer until smooth and creamy. Add sugar and beat for 2 minutes.

3 SLOWLY beat in the eggs, then the apples. Continue beating the mixture on low speed while gradually adding the flour, baking soda, baking powder, salt, and cinnamon. Beat for 2 more minutes.

4 GREASE the 9 x 13-inch baking pan. Spread the mixture into the pan and bake for 30 to 35 minutes, or until a toothpick inserted in the center comes out clean.

Chocolate Abandon

Cooking is like love.
It should be entered into with
abandon or not at all.

—Harriet Van Horne, *Vogue,* 1956

My sister, Debbie, and I were at our Aunt Hazel's for our usual summer visit. The middle of dog days brought nothing more taxing to do than play on the slip-'n-slide and use my cousin Eddie's nice white bedsheet as a gigantic sheet of coloring paper. One day, my aunt came up with a new way to entertain us.

"I'm going to the store. Can you bake this cake while I'm gone?" She pointed to a chocolate cake and frosting mix. "You have baked cakes before, haven't you?"

My older sister said, "Sure, we make cakes all the time."

She told the truth. We had baked many cakes successfully.

Aunt Hazel walked out the door, and my sister, my cousin, and I went into action. Debbie scrutinized the instructions on the back of the box. "Okay, first we have to grease and flour the pans." She assigned that task to my cousin and me. I usually got that sort of job when we baked.

We greased the pans, dumped in flour, and shook them around, dusting the room as much as the pans. It was amazing to see the size of the dust clouds when a pan full of flour makes contact with a porcelain sink.

With each of us taking a turn at the mixer, we somehow finished the batter and dumped it unevenly into the pans. The cake went into the oven.

"Oops! Who forgot to turn on the oven?"

Would the mixture die or implode during the ten minutes the oven needed to preheat? Nothing disastrous happened as the minutes passed, so the cake went back into the oven.

We looked around the shambles we'd made of the kitchen. The white skating rink that was now the kitchen floor had to be swept. We managed to get most of the flour into the dustpan and then into the trash can. The white film that was left behind sort of made the floor look clean.

"Bzzz!" The timer insisted we rescue the cake. When it came from the oven the mouth-watering, gut-wrenching aroma of chocolate cake filled the kitchen.

FUN FACT: Chocolate is made from cocoa, which was discovered by Spanish explorers in 1519 in Mexico.

"Can we eat it now?"

"Yeah, it doesn't have to have frosting."

"I don't think Aunt Hazel would like that."

One of the layers cracked coming out of the pan. That didn't matter. Already deep into the frosting instructions, we forgot about the cake. Cracked cake, smooth cake, it all tasted the same.

"We need margarine."

"Hey, it says here it's got to be soft."

My cousin took a stick from the refrigerator door. "This isn't soft."

"I guess we'll have to go play while it gets soft."

Five minutes later, Debbie said, "I think it's soft enough."

"Hurry, so we'll be done when she gets home."

As if it knew we were in a hurry, the mixer began to slow down. It made a scraping, grinding sound. It moved slower and slower with each passing second. "Whirrr . . . wh . . . ir . . . rrr . . . unh," went the mixer.

"Hey, something smells bad!"

"Yeah, like something burning."

"We'd better turn this thing off."

Debbie scooped a dollop of frosting onto the first layer. It really wasn't a dollop—more a clump. She managed to spread it without destroying the cake. The second layer went on next.

"Better be careful. That's the cracked layer!"

"Look out!"

"It didn't crack all the way through. We can mush it back together! Maybe the frosting will help." She put frosting on top of the cake. It didn't spread. It sort of rolled. Each roll took a huge chunk of cake with it.

"Aunt Hazel's gonna be mad at us."

"She'll think we lied about making cakes."

"We've got to leave it alone and wait until she gets home!"

The aroma of chocolate no longer tantalized. Instead a big, chocolate-scented finger of guilt wafted through the room, poking each of us between the eyes.

Finally, the front door opened and closed. Aunt Hazel's shoes clicked across the hardwood floor of the living room.

"She's home!"

"Here she comes," said Debbie.

Aunt Hazel breezed in, smiling as usual. "It sure smells good in here. So you really do know how to bake a cake."

"The frosting didn't work right," Debbie answered.

"We did it just like the box said," I offered, leaping to my sister's defense.

Aunt Hazel took one look at the slumped and cracked cake and reacted exactly as she had when she found us coloring on Eddie's bedsheet: she burst out laughing.

"Sometimes directions don't work. Let me see what I can do." Her calm voice reassured us.

Well, Aunt Hazel melted some margarine in a saucepan and stirred in the remaining frosting. After stirring for a while, she said, "Well, I think it got too thin." She poured the warm, gooey frosting over the whole cake, letting it run wherever it would. It filled the cracks, covered the lumps, and pooled around the bottom of the plate.

We dug into the best cake ever, realizing that if Aunt Hazel could make a mistake anyone could, and it was all right. Aunt Hazel baked and loved with abandon.

—*Sandra V. McGarrity*

chocolate abandon cake

🛒 INGREDIENTS

- 1 package chocolate cake mix
- 2 3.4 ounce boxes chocolate pudding mix
- 12 ounces milk chocolate chips
- 2 eggs
- 1¾ cups milk
- Butter or vegetable oil for greasing the pan

MAKES
1 BUNDT
CAKE

🍴 TOOLS

Measuring cups

Mixing spoon

Mixing bowl

Bundt pan

Toothpick

Plate

DIRECTIONS

1 **PREHEAT** the oven to 350 degrees.

2 **COMBINE** the cake mix, pudding mix, chocolate chips, eggs, and milk in a mixing bowl and blend well.

3 **GREASE** and flour a Bundt pan and pour the mixture into it.

4 **BAKE** for 50 to 55 minutes or until a toothpick inserted in the center comes out clean.

5 **COOL** in the pan for 15 minutes. Remove the cake from the pan and place it on a plate. Let it cool further before eating.

ENJOY THIS CAKE WITH ABANDON!

#9 **CHOCOLATE PUDDING**—Isn't chocolate pudding the best treat in the world when you're feeling a little sad, bored, or lonely? Doesn't putting the first creamy spoonful into your mouth make you feel like the world is nicer and a little bit sweeter?

Ultimate Granola Brownies

🛒 Ingredients

- ½ cup butter
- 2 cups quick-cooking oats
- 1 cup semisweet chocolate chips
- 1 can (14 ounces) sweetened condensed milk
- ½ cup peanut butter
- 1 egg
- 1 teaspoon baking powder
- ½ teaspoon vanilla extract

🏺 Tools

Saucepan

Mixing bowl

Measuring spoons

Measuring cups

Mixing spoon

Toothpick

9 x 13-inch baking pan

FUN FACT:

Each American eats an average of 51 pounds of chocolate per year.

DIRECTIONS

1 PREHEAT the oven to 350 degrees.

2 MELT the butter in a saucepan, then stir in the oats.

3 SPREAD this mixture evenly into the 9 x 13-inch baking pan.

MAKES
12
BROWNIES

4 BAKE for 15 minutes, and remove the pan from the oven.

5 SPRINKLE the chocolate chips over the warm oatmeal mixture to melt them.

6 IN the mixing bowl, combine the condensed milk, peanut butter, egg, baking powder, and vanilla extract. Smooth this mixture evenly on top of the oatmeal-chocolate mixture.

7 BAKE for another 30 to 35 minutes or until a toothpick inserted in the center comes out clean.

PEANUT BUTTER CUPCAKES

🛒 INGREDIENTS

- 3 tablespoons butter
- ¼ cup peanut butter
- ¼ cup honey
- 1 teaspoon vanilla
- 1 egg
- 1 cup all-purpose flour
- 1 teaspoon baking powder
- ¼ teaspoon salt
- ⅓ cup skim milk

TOOLS

2 large mixing bowls

12 paper muffin cups

Measuring spoons

Measuring cups

Electric mixer

Mixing spoon

Toothpick

Muffin tin

MAKES
12
CUPCAKES

DiReCTiONS

1 PREhEaT the oven to 350 degrees.

2 IN a large mixing bowl, cream together the butter, peanut butter, honey, and vanilla with an electric hand mixer.

3 SLOWLY add the egg; mix for 1 minute.

4 IN another mixing bowl, combine the flour, baking powder, and salt. Slowly add this to the creamed mixture, alternating with the skim milk and mixing on low speed until all the ingredients are combined.

5 LiNE the muffin tin with the paper muffin cups and fill them three-quarters full.

6 BaKE for 15 to 20 minutes or until a toothpick inserted in the center of a cupcake comes out clean.

> **VARIATION:**
> After pouring into muffin pans, spoon 1 teaspoon of jelly or jam of your choice into the batter before baking.

#10 cUPCaK.E—I'm not talking about the perfect kind of cupcake that you can buy at a store. I like the kind your mom makes for your birthday party, then covers with sprinkles. Cupcakes can be lopsided or missing a few little edges. They're often chocolatey-brown, but they can be yellow, blue, or green if you like to mess around with food colorings. No matter what color they are, cupcakes always feel like a party.

Don't Touch The Dough!

I t was Christmas, and magic was in the air. My three sons—John, Mike, and Rob—were filled with excitement. Although they were all under the age of ten, they were old enough to know about the wonders of Christmas and anticipate all the joys of the season. They wanted to decorate everything in the house. They wanted to decorate the outside of the house and the yard. They even wanted to decorate the dogs! Not a good idea. Dogs don't like to be decorated. But most especially, they wanted to bake special Christmas cookies.

Now, I am not a baker. I love to cook, but when it comes to baking I am not really good. Most of my baking experiences started with a box or a mix. Nothing fancy. None of this starting from scratch for me. *But how hard could it be?* And my little boys were just so excited, I couldn't say no.

I found a recipe for basic butter cookie dough. The recipe promised light, flaky, and buttery cookies. It looked simple enough. The boys and I went to the store and bought cookie cutters in every Christmas shape available. Then we went to the market and bought all the necessary ingredients. We also bought lots and lots of decorations for our cookies. And sprinkles—don't forget the sprinkles. We would make the most beautiful and delicious cookies ever!

Mixing the dough didn't seem too hard. I mean you measure the ingredients, put them in a bowl, and mix. The boys all took turns measuring and mixing. Flour, sugar, and salt went all over the kitchen—some of it even got into the mixing bowl. The recipe said to work quickly and not handle the dough too much. I wasn't quite sure why. I mean, the more you mix it the better it must be. And why did they state that the dough must be chilled—and thoroughly? Obviously, the creator of this particular recipe didn't have kids. Had he or she ever worked with three young boys who weren't really good about waiting? But we did divide the dough into three disks and chilled it for a while. Things were going well.

Finally, the dough was chilled. Now it was time to get to work and make those fabulous cookies. We floured the board and started to roll out the dough. The recipe said to roll the dough to a thickness of "¼ inch" but not to let it get too warm. So how do you roll the dough, cut the cookies, and transfer them to the cookie sheets without letting the dough get too warm? Simple—as I was to find out—you don't! It's not possible. The boys cut out the shapes with our new cookie cutters, but before I could transfer them to the cookie sheet, the dough got too warm and stuck to the board. As I tried to move the cookies, they lost all of their fabulous Christmas shapes and became mushy lumps. Santa's head fell off, and Rudolph's nose and three of his legs didn't make it. *Help!* This was not working at all. The boys were not happy, and I was a mess. Wasn't this supposed to be fun?

Okay, let's try again. We chilled the dough and, in a while, tried again. This time things went from bad to worse. I was frantic. I was like a drill sergeant. "Hurry!" "Go faster!" "No laughing, this is serious." We had to move fast before the dough came up to room temperature—again. We rolled, and the boys cut the shapes. All the while I was telling them, "Try not to touch the dough." "Don't touch the dough." "Don't TOUCH the DOUGH." "DON'T TOUCH THE DOUGH!!" Failed again. Droopy cookie dough all over the place. What is a mother to do? What good did my university degree do if I couldn't even make cookies with my kids?

Right about this time my husband, Frank, came home from work. Now Frank can boil water, but he doesn't cook. He saw the mess in the kitchen, saw his wife and three boys covered in flour, and heard me yelling, "Don't touch the dough!" So he did the best thing he could have done. He quietly dusted the flour off me, took me by the hand, removed me from the kitchen, and closed the door. Then he and the boys started the cookie experience all over again. Sometime later, after I stopped mumbling and grumbling, I heard some very interesting sounds coming from the kitchen. Laughter? Yes, it had to be laughter. Frank not only took charge of baking the cookies—he turned the whole experience into magic for the boys.

The cookies were delicious and decorated beautifully. The sprinkles twinkled. Rudolph's nose was red. The kids were so happy and proud of the job they had done. And Frank, well, he not only rescued me but also the Christmas season. From that year on, until John, Mike, and Rob had grown up and moved out, we baked Christmas cookies. Well, not exactly "we." The boys baked—but not with me. They baked with Frank. Each year, right after Thanksgiving, all of the "men" in my life would make a Christmas cookie baking date. It was a date they all looked forward to. I, on the other hand, was encouraged to "Make other plans!"

—*Barbara LoMonaco*

Peanut Butter Playdough

My parents always told me not to play with my food, but here's a food kids should play with!

 Ingredients

- 1½ cups smooth peanut butter
- 6 tablespoons honey
- ½ cup dry milk powder

Tools

Bowl

Measuring cups

Measuring spoons

Serves 2

Directions

1 **COMBINE** the peanut butter, honey, and milk powder in a bowl.

2 **ROLL** out this mixture with your hands (yes, your hands), adding more dry milk to prevent stickiness.

3 **NOW** the dough's ready to use! Have fun and make whatever your heart desires. You can use confectioners' sugar to prevent the playdough from sticking to the board or table.

Chocolate Dippers

 Ingredients

- 3 cups chocolate chips

- 3 tablespoons vegetable oil

- Pretzels, potato chips, strawberries (well dried), apricots, marshmallows, or cookies for dippers

Tools

Baking sheet pan

Waxed paper

Mixing cups

Microwave-safe bowl

Microwave

Mixing spoon

DIRECTIONS

1 **LINE** a baking sheet pan with waxed paper.

2 **PUT** chocolate and oil into the microwave-safe bowl and, stirring every 10 seconds until the chips are melted, place the bowl in the microwave. Remove the mixture from the microwave. The chocolate is now ready for dipping.

3 **DIP** whatever you'd like into the chocolate! As you finish each item, place it on the baking sheet pan.

4 **REFRIGERATE** the dippers until the chocolate is hard.

> 💡 **TIP:**
> You also can eat these while the
> chocolate is still warm and gooey!
> You make the rules!

THE GRANDMA HANDS

Airiana, my five-year-old granddaughter, was helping me make cookies one day. When it was time to remove them from the oven Airiana pleaded with me to let her do it.

Concerned that she might burn herself, I told her, "I'll remove them from the oven, but you may help me remove them from the cookie sheet and decorate them."

"Please, Grandma," she pleaded. "I won't burn myself if I use the Grandma hands!"

"No, sweetie, it's too risky," I replied as I wondered what she meant by "Grandma hands."

"Pretty please, Grandma. I'll be really careful! Can I get the Grandma hands?" she begged.

Puzzled, I asked, "Can you get the what?"

She ran over to the drawer where I keep my pot holders, took out two oven mitts, placed them on her tiny hands, looked up, and smiled. "Grandma hands!" she said.

—*Christine M. Smith*

I'M a BaKER, Too

Dirt on my face,

Mud on my shoes,

Mom's pots and pans,

A dessert made for two,

A sprinkle of rocks,

Like candy and icing Momma puts on her cake,

I added a few leaves using Papa's rake,

All this blended to make a special treat,

When I go in to give it to Momma,

I better remember to wipe my feet.

—*Tanya Lyles*

Final Thoughts

Culinary Memories

Think of the adventures you will have in the kitchen cooking these recipes and creating some of your own.

I have truly loved gathering these stories and recipes, and I am glad I had the opportunity to share them with you. These stories and recipes provide the basics for cooking. Fall in love with cooking and share it with someone close to you.

Join with me, and bring families back into the kitchen where they can talk together, eat together, and enjoy each other's company. Learn how to measure and how to cook, but, most important, have fun! I was fortunate enough to be around a family who loved food. I hope that everyone can be as fortunate. Let's get back into the kitchen, learn how to cook, cook up a storm, and create your own culinary memories.

If you want to have more fun, you can join our community by visiting www.antoniofrontera.com, and find more recipes, enjoy amazing games, and discover Antonio's secret cooking tips.

Cooking is fun! Cooking is love. What else can I say– Cooking is Chicken Soup for the Soul.

—Chef Antonio Frontera

Who is Jack Canfield?

Jack Canfield is the cocreator and editor of the *Chicken Soup for the Soul* series, which *Time* magazine has called "the publishing phenomenon of the decade." The series now has more than 140 titles with over 100 million copies in print in forty-seven languages. Jack is also the coauthor of eight other bestselling books including *The Success Principles™: How to Get from Where You Are to Where You Want to Be, Dare to Win, The Aladdin Factor, You've Got to Read This Book,* and *The Power of Focus: How to Hit Your Business, Personal and Financial Targets with Absolute Certainty.*

Jack has recently developed a telephone coaching program and an online coaching program based on his most recent book *The Success Principles.* He also offers a seven-day Breakthrough to Success seminar every summer, which attracts 400 people from fifteen countries around the world.

Jack is the CEO of Chicken Soup for the Soul Enterprises and the Canfield Training Group in Santa Barbara, California, and founder of the Foundation for Self-Esteem in Culver City, California. He has conducted intensive personal and professional development seminars on the principles of success for more than a million people in twenty-nine countries around the world. Jack is a dynamic keynote speaker and he has spoken to hundreds of thousands of others at more than 1,000 corporations, universities, professional conferences and conventions, and has been seen by millions more on national television shows such as *Oprah, Montel, The Today Show, Larry King Live, Fox and Friends, Inside Edition, Hard Copy, CNN's Talk Back Live, 20/20, Eye to Eye,* and the *NBC Nightly News* and the *CBS Evening News.* Jack was also a featured teacher on the hit movie *The Secret.*

Jack is the recipient of many awards and honors, including three honorary doctorates and a Guinness World Records Certificate for having seven books from the *Chicken Soup for the Soul* series appearing on *The New York Times* bestseller list on May 24, 1998.

To write to Jack or for inquiries about Jack as a speaker, his coaching programs, trainings or seminars, use the following contact information:

Jack Canfield
The Canfield Companies
P.O. Box 30880 • Santa Barbara, CA 93130
phone: 805-563-2935 • fax: 805-563-2945
E-mail: info4jack@jackcanfield.com
www.jackcanfield.com

Who Is Mark Victor Hansen?

In the area of human potential, no one is more respected than Mark Victor Hansen. For more than thirty years, Mark has focused solely on helping people from all walks of life reshape their personal vision of what's possible. His powerful messages of possibility, opportunity, and action have created powerful change in thousands of organizations and millions of individuals worldwide.

He is a sought-after keynote speaker, bestselling author, and marketing maven. Mark's credentials include a lifetime of entrepreneurial success and an extensive academic background. He is a prolific writer with many bestselling books, such as *The One Minute Millionaire, Cracking the Millionaire Code, How to Make the Rest of Your Life the Best of Your Life, The Power of Focus, The Aladdin Factor,* and *Dare to Win,* in addition to the Chicken Soup for the Soul series. Mark has had a profound influence on many people through his library of audios, videos, and articles in the areas of big thinking, sales achievement, wealth building, publishing success, and personal and professional development.

Mark is the founder of the MEGA Seminar Series. MEGA Book Marketing University and Building Your MEGA Speaking Empire are annual conferences where Mark coaches and teaches new and aspiring authors, speakers, and experts on building lucrative publishing and speaking careers. Other MEGA events include MEGA Info-Marketing and My MEGA Life.

He has appeared on *Oprah*, CNN, and *The Today Show*. He has been quoted in *Time, U.S. News & World Report, USA Today, The New York Times,* and *Entrepreneur*. In countless radio interviews, he has assured our planet's people that "you can easily create the life you deserve."

As a philanthropist and humanitarian, Mark works tirelessly for organizations such as Habitat for Humanity, American Red Cross, March of Dimes, Childhelp USA, and many others. He is the recipient of numerous awards that honor his entrepreneurial spirit, philanthropic heart, and business acumen. He is a lifetime member of the Horatio Alger Association of Distinguished Americans, an organization that honored Mark with the prestigious Horatio Alger Award for his extraordinary life achievements.

Mark Victor Hansen is an enthusiastic crusader of what's possible and is driven to make the world a better place.

Mark Victor Hansen & Associates, Inc.
P.O. Box 7665 • Newport Beach, CA 92658
phone: 949-764-2640 • fax: 949-722-6912
website: www.markvictorhansen.com

Who is Chef Antonio?

At the age of eight, after being given a working toy oven, Antonio Frontera started cooking meals for his entire family. At the age of fifteen, while working at the beautiful Country Inn Restaurant overlooking West Point and the Hudson River, he knew he wanted to make cooking his career. Soon after high school, Antonio applied to the Culinary Institute of America and was accepted.

Two years later, Antonio graduated with a Foodservice and Culinary Arts cooking degree. Since then, Antonio has owned and worked at four-star restaurants, delis, cafés, and pastry shops. Among other activities, he has performed live cooking shows in his restaurant studio, enhanced the quality of restaurants with local farm-grown products, and designed international cuisine services. His work has earned him glowing write-ups in local and national magazines, newspapers, and college-based publications.

Antonio recently sold his eclectic deli, which was highly regarded by the Vassar College community. Antonio is hard at work on a number of books, including two children's books, a humorous storybook/cookbook, and a healthy-lifestyle cookbook. To top it all off, he has also been working to develop a kids' cooking show (among others) for television. You can visit him at his website, http://www.antoniofrontera.com, or at a school near you where he will be showing the kids of tomorrow about cooking.

SUPPORTING OTHERS

The coauthors of *Chicken Soup for the Soul Kids in the Kitchen* have selected Free the Children to receive a portion of the book's proceeds.

Free the Children is the world's largest network of children helping children through education. Through our organization's unique youth-driven approach, more than one million young people have been involved in our innovative programs in more than forty-five countries. Founded in 1995 by international child rights activist Craig Kielburger when he was twelve years old, Free the Children has an established track record of success, with three nominations for the Nobel Peace Prize and partnerships with the United Nations and Oprah's Angel Network. Craig received the 2006 World Children's Prize for the Rights of the Child, also known as the Children's Nobel Peace Prize.

- Free the Children has built more than 450 primary schools in developing countries—that's enough schools to give 40,000 children the chance to go to school.
- Free the Children also helps improve the lives of children and their families so that they're healthy, eat nutritious food, and don't have to work, so they can go to school ready to learn. Free the Children has sent $11 million in medical supplies; given out more than 20,500 school and health kits; created health-care products that have helped 505,000; and set up alternative income projects that have empowered more than 22,500 women and their families.

To learn more, please visit:

Free the Children International Office
233 Carlton Street
Toronto, Ontario M5A 2L2
Canada

Free the Children U.S.A.
P.O. Box 32099
Hartford, Connecticut 06150-2099
U.S.A.

Tele: 1.416.925.5894 • Fax: 1.416.925.8242

www.freethechildren.com • info@freethechildren.com

CONTRIBUTORS

Suzanne Baginskie recently retired from her job of more then twenty-five years as a law office manager/paralegal. She has been published in other Chicken Soup for the Soul books, *Cat's Magazine,* and *True Romance,* and she has published several nonfiction articles. She lives on the west coast of Florida with her husband, Al.

Aaron Bacall has graduate degrees in organic chemistry as well as in educational administration and supervision from New York University. He has been a pharmaceutical research chemist, college department coordinator, instructor in college, and cartoonist. He has sold his cartoons to most national publications and has had several books of his cartoons published. Three of his cartoons are featured in the permanent collection at the Harvard Business School's Baker Library. He continues to create and sell his cartoons and is writing a book. He can be reached at abacall@msn.com.

Jo Rae Cash is not a country-western singer. She is a freelance writer and mother of two teenagers who give her plenty to wail about. In addition to writing, Jo Rae enjoys tennis, gardening, and tea. Jo Rae resides in Simpsonville, South Carolina, and can be contacted at t4me@bellsouth.com.

Bailey Corona is a fourth-grader at Legacy Private Academy. He loves playing outside with his friends. His love for sports continues to grow. This year he made AYSO all-stars for soccer.

Andrew J. Corsa is a graduate student in philosophy at Syracuse University. In addition to working on academic essays, Andrew has cowritten a children's book and several cooking shows with Chef Antonio Frontera. Andrew is also the author of several works of science fiction. His website can be found at http://writersthoughts.com/Corsa.

Angela Thieman Dino is an anthropologist living in Denver, Colorado, with her magical husband Brian, son Dante, and daughter Lia. She thanks her own mother, LeAnn, and mother-in-law, Shirley, for blessing their families with such abundant love and good food! Mange, mange!

Joanne L. Faries is from North Wales, Pennsylvania. She has a business degree from Temple University and an MBA from UTA. In 2005, she threw away her red stapler to concentrate on writing. Her understanding husband hopes she learns to cook better. Joanne is working on a book of short stories.

Tessa Floehr received her M.Ed. from the University of Dayton. She is currently teaching preschool and establishing a writing career. She enjoys spending time in the kitchen with her daughters, Sophia and Amelia. Together they have concocted several original recipes and enjoyed many special cooking moments together. You can contact her at tessa@floehr.com.

Sally Friedman is a graduate of the University of Pennsylvania and has been a freelance writer for over three decades. Her work has frequently appeared in the Chicken Soup series, as well as in newspapers and magazines around the United States. She is the mother of three daughters and the grandmother of seven spectacular grandchildren. Her e-mail address is pinegander@aol.com.

Valeri Frontera was born in Newburgh, New York, in the 1940s and is married with four children and four grandchildren. She has always loved to cook and involve her children in cooking and baking. She is proud to say that two of her children went on to the Culinary Institute of America and later opened a resturant where she and her husband lent a hand.

Pamela Hackett Hobson is a wife, mother of Tom and Mike, and author of two novels—*The Bronxville Book Club* and *The Silent Auction*—featured in *The New York Times* article "Buzzzz, Murmurs Follow Novel." To learn more about the author and her writing projects, visit www.pamelahobson.com or send an e-mail to author@pamelahobson.com.

Linda S. Handiak is a teacher and translator in Montreal, Quebec. She has volunteered abroad for restoration and conservation projects and has published several travel articles.

Jonny Hawkins's cartoons have appeared in over 350 publications, over 100 books, and in his own cartoon-a-day calendars over the last twenty years. His latest book, *The Awesome Book of Healthy Humor,* is available everywhere. He lives in Sherwood, MI, with his wife, Carissa, and their three children, Nate, Zach, and Kara, to whom he delightfully dedicates these cartoons. He can be reached at jonnyhawkins2nz@yahoo.com.

Robyn Henry is a freelance designer. Presently, she is working in various techniques in kiln-fired glass and metal. Her long-time interest has been in writing prose and poetry. Her more recent endeavor is getting a closer look at flowers through macrophotography and combining words with images.

Catherine Inscore received her associate's degree in liberal arts from Copper Mountain College, a local community college in Joshua Tree, California. It was through a school assignment that this piece was written. Catherine has given birth to seven children and has inherited six more through her second marriage to husband Barry Inscore. They share an abundance of grandchildren—twenty-two to be exact. Catherine works for Copper Mountain College, in the Greenleaf Library, as a library specialist. Please e-mail her at c_j_inscore@yahoo.com.

Jennie Ivey lives in Cookeville, Tennessee. She is a columnist for the *Cookeville Herald-Citizen* newspaper and the coauthor of two books—*Tennessee Tales the Textbooks Don't Tell* and *E Is for Elvis.* She can be contacted at jivey@frontiernet.net.

Mimi Greenwood Knight is a freelance writer living in Folsom, Louisiana, with her husband, David, and their four children—Haley, Molly, Hewson, and Jonah—and four dogs, four cats, and one chuckle-headed bird. She enjoys Bible study and butterfly gardening, baking, and the lost art of letter writing. She can be reached via e-mail at djknight@airmail.net.

T. Jensen Lacey is the author of six books, a young adult novel, and more than 700 articles in newspapers and magazines. Her writing and photography have garnered national and international awards. This is her fifth story to appear in the Chicken Soup for the Soul series. See her website at www.TJensenLacey.com.

Sharon L. Landeen is a retired elementary-school teacher. She still enjoys working with youth as a 4-H leader (for more than twenty years) and as a reading mentor and art teacher at a local school. She also serves on the board of the Society of Southwestern Authors and is an avid University of Arizona sports fan and an active grandma.

Delores Liesner is an inspirational writer and speaker from Racine, Wisconsin, who recently completed a 126-page cancer information, resource, and recipe book—*Eating with Dave: A Healthy Response to a Cancer Diagnosis*—inspired by her grandson. Delores finds joy in her abundant life as wife, mom, and grandmother. Contact her at delores7faith@yahoo.com.

Barbara LoMonaco received her bachelor of science degree from the University of Southern California and has an elementary teaching credential. Barbara has worked for Chicken Soup for the Soul since February 1998 as its story acquisitions manager.

Amy Luciano received her bachelor of arts degree in English from Chaminade University in Hawaii. She is the inventor of EYE-SMILER® and is currently working on various screen-writing projects and hopes eventually to contribute to shows that will make television more inspirational.

Tanya Lyles spends her spare time writing. She likes to share her thoughts and inspirations with others. Tanya has published poetry, as well as an illustrated children's book coming out soon. She likes to get lost in her work, entering into the world that exists only in her thoughts and expressions.

Sandra V. McGarrity is a writer whose work has appeared in many story compilations and magazines. She is the author of three novels. Visit her website at hometown.aol.com/mygr 8m8/myhomepage/books.html.

Linda Kaullen Perkins has had ninety-five short stories, articles, and essays appear in various publications. After many years in education, she now spends her days writing and enjoying the farm with her husband and pets. Check out her webpage: http://hometown. aol.com/squatters5/lindakaullenperkins.html.

Helen Kay Polaski is a freelance writer and book editor. Her work has appeared in various newspapers, books, and newsletters.

Carol McAdoo Rehme was once "Mommy" to four preschoolers and is now "Grammy" to three. She finds herself—once again—in the kitchen. A reluctant cook, Carol is coauthor of the upcoming *Chicken Soup for the Empty Nester's Soul*. She also directs a nonprofit named Vintage Voices, Inc., which takes interactive arts programs to the frail elderly. You can contact her at carol@rehme.com; her website can be found at www.rehme.com.

Bruce Robinson is an award-winning internationally published cartoonist whose work has appeared in numerous consumer and trade periodicals such as the *National Enquirer, The Saturday Evening Post, Woman's World, The Sun, First,* and *Highlights for Children.* He is also author of the cartoon book *Good Medicine.* Contact him at cartoonsbybruce robinson@hotmail.com.

Paula L. Silici is an award-winning, multipublished author. She firmly believes in the dictum "Peace begins with me" and endeavors to practice at least one random act of kindness every day. She also fully understands that our precious children will someday run the world. You can reach her at psilici@hotmail.com.

Gail Small is a Fulbright Memorial Scholar and a People to People Ambassador. She is listed in *Who's Who Among America's Universities* and in *Who's Who Among America's Teachers.* Please e-mail this educator of thirty-five years, consultant, author, and motivational speaker at JoyforGail@aol.com. Learn more about this five-times-published author at http://GailSmall.com.

Christine M. Smith is a mother of three, grandmother of thirteen, and foster mother to many. She and her husband, James, have been married for thirty-eight years and reside in Atoka, Oklahoma. Christine loves family, reading, writing, and sharing Christ's love with others. Please e-mail her at iluvmyfamilyxxx000@yahoo.com.

Jennifer Smith teaches high school in a boarding academy for at-risk teenagers. God has blessed her writing adventures with two of her stories published in the Chicken Soup for the Soul series and her first children's book, *Things I Wonder.* Check out her book at www.hisworkpub.com or e-mail her at happilyeverafter2004@yahoo.com.

Cristy Trandahl has been a teacher and a writer for the nation's leading student-monitoring testing company. Most recently, Cristy has contributed to *Cup of Comfort for Mothers to Be, Chicken Soup for the Soul: Recipes for Busy Moms, Chicken Soup for the Shoppers' Soul, Dust and Fire: Twenty Years of Women's Stories,* and *Teacher Miracles.* Cristy, her husband, and six children live in rural Minnesota. Visit her at www.cristytrandahl.com.

Gillian White is an author and "shepherd" of projects—both literary and otherwise—and endeavors to support worthy ventures. Her literary endeavors include *Life Lessons for Busy Moms: 7 Essential Ingredients to Organize and Balance Your World, The Senior Organizer and BioBinder,* and *Cherished Memories: The Story of My Life* (http://delphihealthprod-ucts.com). Her philanthropic endeavors include http://Waterkeeper.org, http://EBkids.org, www.Eliyah.com, and http://Vitaloptions.org.

Lois June Wickstrom is a children's author. You can visit her websites at www.lochness-monster.com and www.reluctantspy.com. She enjoys writing, reading, gardening, and traveling to strange places, foreign and domestic, with her husband. Please e-mail her at reluctantspy@gmail.com.

Mark Wilk graduated Vassar College in 2005 with a B.A. in Film. He is an avid pianist and composer, and is currently co-writing (with singer/comedienne Marilyn Michaels) the book and lyrics to a new musical, *Alyss,* based upon Lewis Carroll's *Alice in Wonderland.*

PERMISSIONS

Spilled Milk. Reprinted by permission of Helen Kay Polaski. ©2006 Helen Kay Polaski.

Children Grieve, Too. Reprinted by permission of Jennie Ivey. ©2006 Jennie Ivey.

Cooking Outdoors. Reprinted by permission of Lois June Wickstrom. ©2006 Lois June Wickstrom.

Delicate Food. Reprinted by permission of Joanne Lee Faries. ©2006 Joanne Lee Faries.

Snow and Soup. Reprinted by permission of Andrew J. Corsa. ©2005 Andrew J. Corsa.

Knickknacks. Reprinted by permission of Amy Luciano. ©2006 Amy Luciano.

The Legacy of Pizza Crackers. Reprinted by permission of Jennifer Smith. ©2006 Jennifer Smith.

Sharing the Dough. Reprinted by permission of Carol D. Rehme. ©2006 Carol D. Rehme.

A Surprising Trophy. Reprinted by permission of Suzanne Baginskie. ©2006 Suzanne Baginskie.

Nona's Garden. Reprinted by permission of Paula L. Silici. ©2000 Paula L. Silici.

The Royal Baker and Pasties. Reprinted by permission of Delores Fae Liesner. ©2006 Delores Fae Liesner.

Love Soup Emergency. Reprinted by permission of Cristy Trandahl. ©2006 Cristy Trandahl.

Seeing Eyes Mom. Reprinted by permission of Carol D. Rehme. ©2006 Carol D. Rehme.

Chinese Pizza. Reprinted by permission of Pamela Hackett Hobson. ©2006 Pamela Hackett Hobson.

Snow Memories. Reprinted by permission of Valeri Frontera. ©2005 Valeri Frontera.

"But I Don't Like Tomatoes!" Reprinted by permission of Gillian White. ©2006 Gillian White.

Never Too Messy. Reprinted by permission of Angela Thieman Dino. ©2007 Angela Thieman Dino.

Beating the System. Reprinted by permission of Sally Friedman. ©2006 Sally Friedman.

Little Man Cody Cookies. Reprinted by permission of Sharon Lee Landeen. ©2006 Sharon Lee Landeen.

Milk and Cookies. Reprinted by permission of Gail Endelman Small. ©2006 Gail Endelman Small.

The Spice of Life. Reprinted by permission of Linda S. Handiak. ©2006 Linda S. Handiak.

Thanks to our Models

Thank you to Young Chefs Academy for providing us with a fun, colorful setting to photograph some of our models for the book.

A big thanks to our young chefs, who were always energized, ready to cook, have fun and take a lot of pictures: Emily Bayne, Alivia Brower, Bella Chitty, Hannah Chitty, Michael Adam Cornette, Nicole Elizabeth Cornette, Shauna Dowling, Jordan Durham, Tyrese Franklin, Gianna Marie Frontera, Melchiorre Frontera, Cole Higgins, Emma Merritt, Justin Merritt, Lydia Merritt, Blake Oldfield, Kylie Oldfield, Conor Parnell, Logan Parnell, Corey Phelps, Braydn Pierce, Ashleigh Marie Rahuba, Matthew Tyler Rahuba, Tomy Reeves, Lauren Rick, Emily Thorne, Brandon Waller, Tyler Walsh, and Isaac White.

Come discover a cooking school created just for kids!

Join thousands of children across the US and Canada who are cooking up some fun at Young Chefs Academy.

Come on into our kitchen where kids learn the basics of cooking, and learn that cooking can be quite creative, full of discovery, and a whole lot of fun!

To find a Young Chefs Academy near you or for franchise information, visit their website:

http://www.youngchefsacademy.com

INDEX